The Humanist Way

Other Books by Edward L. Ericson

AMERICAN FREEDOM AND THE RADICAL RIGHT
THE FREE MIND THROUGH THE AGES

(as editor)
EMERSON ON TRANSCENDENTALISM

The Humanist Way

*An Introduction to
Ethical Humanist Religion*

Edward L. Ericson

Foreword by Isaac Asimov

A Frederick Ungar Book
CONTINUUM ● NEW YORK

1988

The Continuum Publishing Company
370 Lexington Avenue
New York, NY 10017

Printed in the United States of America

Library of Congress Cataloging-in-Publication Data

Ericson, Edward L.
    The humanist way: an introduction to ethical humanist religion /
Edward L. Ericson.
        p.   cm.
    Bibliography: p.
    Includes index.
    ISBN 0-8044-2176-5
    1. American Ethical Union.   2. Ethical Culture movement.
3. Humanism.   4. Secularism.   I. Title.
BJ11.A63E75 1988
171'.2—dc19   87-27348
                                                     CIP

Contents

Foreword

by Isaac Asimov

Edward L. Ericson was born in Florida in 1929. Recently he returned to Florida to devote full time to writing, so that, in a sense, Florida has given and Florida has taken away.

But of course he has not been truly taken away, not yet, for he has spent his entire life in a true devotion to the various facets of Humanism, and that continues, of course, for in his native "retreat" he has not abated one jot of his activities. (Some people are like that.)

He began his formal work in the cause as a Unitarian minister in Oregon and in Virginia, and in 1959 entered the Ethical Culture movement as Leader of the Washington (D.C.) Ethical Society. That continued for twelve years and in 1971 he joined the Board of Leaders of the New York Ethical Culture Society. In 1974, he served as acting Chairman of the Board and the next year he became Chairman. He received numerous awards along the way.

My own association with Ed Ericson came about as follows:

In the year 1973, Janet Jeppson and I wished to be married in order to attach the odor of legality (if not sanctity) to an attachment that we knew already existed firmly in our hearts. We were not children at the time, I was 53-years old, a professor of biochemistry and a writer; and she was 47, a psychiatrist, psychoanalyst, and a writer. We were both thoroughgoing Humanists and knew what we wanted and didn't want.

We wanted a legal marriage and we didn't want the irrelevance of a religious ritual. On the other hand, neither did we want the clamminess of City Hall. Janet therefore suggested Ethical Culture and sought out Ed Ericson, as an appropriate intermediary in the process, since he and I were both signatories of "Humanist Manifesto II."

We were married in Janet's living room on November 30, 1973, with Ed officiating and with two friends, Alfred and Phyllis Balk, as witnesses. Afterward, the five of us went out for a wedding dinner at a Chinese restaurant and joy was unconfined. The deed was done our way—without orange blossoms, without formal symbolism, without useless gowns and tuxedos, without incense or organ music or meaningless traditions. Just with a great deal of satisfaction that we could add the necessary minimum formality with a minimum fuss to what was already maximum reality. To us, this was the Humanist way.

Janet and I responded to the event in different, but very similar ways. Janet joined the Ethical Culture Society, and I have somehow become president of the American Humanist Association.

We are still married, of course, since Ed Ericson assured me (in response to my anxious questioning) that his departure from New York in no way invalidated the ceremony. What's more, we will stay married, I am quite confident, "till death do us part," even though we did not listen to anyone sing "Oh, Promise Me." That's the Humanist way.

But, of course, there is a great deal more that is decent, sensible, and civilized to the Humanist way. It does not simply apply to personal matters; it is also a view of the world, of each person's relation to other people, of the unity of humanity, of its place in the whole fabric of life against the background of our planet and our universe, of—but read Ed's book, now in your hand, and see.

Introductory Note on Secular and Religious Humanism

Humanism, in the context of this study, affirms the freedom, dignity, and well-being of human beings as the supreme object of the moral life, without belief in any supernatural power or being. It is committed to the pursuit of the human good as the ultimate value of this life—which Humanists believe is the only life we have reason to expect. On these basic tenets "religious" Humanists and "secular" (nonreligious) Humanists are agreed. While some religious Humanists retain a conception of God as a symbolic representation of the highest moral and spiritual values, many others feel that "God language" is misleading and inappropriate for a religious philosophy that rejects the concept of the supernatural. (Still others follow Spinoza's example of equating God with nature or the cosmos, conceived as an impersonal, eternally existing reality.)

The sole disagreement between religious Humanists and most secular Humanists is whether or not a purely nontheistic belief (a belief not involving the doctrine of a purposive, supernatural God) can properly be considered a religion. Religious Humanists affirm that it can, pointing out that the only universal characteristic of religion, common to all traditions, is a sense of the sacred, which in all but the most primitive cults involves moral and spiritual commitment. Albert Schweitzer's inspired phrase, "reverence for life," sums up the religious Humanist's attitude toward existence.

Sir Julian Huxley, the recent evolutionary biologist and religious Humanism's most eminent and tireless champion of this century, wrote: "We are perforce monists, in the sense of believers in the oneness of things; we see ourselves, together with our science and our beliefs, as an integral part of the cosmic process, instead of outside it."

Like the American philosopher, John Dewey, Huxley found the essence of the religious life within the transforming quality of human experience. In his essay, "The New Divinity," Sir Julian observed: "For want of a better term, I use the term *divine*, though this quality of divinity is not truly supernatural but *transnatural*—it grows out of ordinary nature, but transcends it. The divine is what man finds worthy of adoration, that which compels his awe." The close affinity between ethical and religious feeling is suggested by Huxley's formulation.

This study is offered primarily as an introduction to Ethical Humanism as that religious philosophy exists in the Ethical Culture societies (the American Ethical Union). But I have also kept in view those who belong to other historically related liberal religious and Humanist movements, or who individually subscribe to similar beliefs. Throughout, I have tried to show how these groups have influenced each other for more than a century. Other Humanist bodies in North America include the American Humanist Association, the Fellowship of Religious Humanists, the Society for Humanistic Judaism, and many of the churches and fellowships of the Unitarian Universalist Association, whose membership and ministry contain many avowed nontheistic Humanists.

In this overview of the Humanist movement, we are concerned primarily with basic principles and long-term developments. However, the current controversy created by Fundamentalist misrepresentations about the alleged "religion of secular humanism" requires a preliminary comment to be dealt with more fully later in this study.

Having no God to propitiate, nontheistic religious devotion is directed toward other ethical and spiritual ends. In a footnote to a 1961 Supreme Court decision that extended the full protection of the freedom of religion clause of the First Amendment to a nontheistic Ethical Humanist (a member of the Washington, D.C., Ethical Society), Justice Hugo Black observed:

> Among religions in this country which do not teach what would generally be considered a belief in God are Buddhism, Taoism, Ethical Culture, Secular Humanism and others.

The decision in this case (*Torcaso v. Watkins*) held that a nontheist is entitled to the same rights of conscience under the Constitution as a believer in God. The Court did not "establish" Humanism as the preferred religion of the secular state as some right-wing Catholic and Fundamentalist polemicists have since absurdly contended. The Court only assured to Ethical Humanists and other nontheists the same rights that Baptists, Lutherans, Catholics, and other religious citizens have always claimed for themselves. A contrary decision would have reduced Humanists and all other nontheists to second-class citizens whose full liberty of conscience would be infringed upon. (The government's refusal for many years to accept nontheists as conscientious objectors under the military draft resulted in prison terms for many—a grievous example of religious discrimination on the basis of theology.)

Unfortunately, in the footnote quoted above, Justice Black did not help to clarify matters by referring to Humanist religion as "Secular Humanism." The use of this combination of terms in the Supreme Court's Torcaso decision has since confused the distinction between the secular and religious types of Humanism.

The confusion came about in the following manner. Shortly before the Supreme Court heard the Torcaso case, a congregation of religious Humanists in California had won in state courts their claim to be a church, a decision that was argued in the Torcaso case as a precedent. Unfortunately, a legal brief that cited the precedent referred to the California congregation as "Secular Humanists," an ambiguous and problematic conjunction of terms to use when referring to a religious body. But Justice Black apparently accepted the label as an accurate and usual designation, and the practice ever since of identifying Humanist religion as "Secular Humanism" has stirred endless misunderstanding and befuddled public comprehension!

Fundamentalist zealots have exploited the resultant confusion to claim that "the religion of secular humanism" (*sic*) is being taught in the public schools. The charge is wholly frivolous and based solely on different applications of the word Humanist. If the accusation *were* true, religious and secular Humanists would be among those most alarmed and aggrieved, since Humanists are ardent in defense of the constitutional principle of church-state separation. Humanists do not want the state to get into the business of sponsoring or interpreting the "true" meaning of religion, regardless of the interpretation that might be favored. Religious Humanists, like other Americans who cherish free religion in a free society, seek only the right to advocate and practice their Humanist faith as private citizens and in their voluntary associations.

On the other hand, the purely secular aspects of Humanist philosophy coincide precisely with the democratic ideals and scientific methods of thought that constitute the foundation of contemporary free society; and, indeed, they spring from the same historical and intellectual sources.

Fundamentalist claimants have simply put the cart before the horse. Respect for the scientific method and commitment to free, unfettered inquiry are not "dogmas of Humanism" imposed on contemporary education and society. Humanists, like others, accept these approaches as the practical, time-tested methods of discovery and self-correction.

Nonreligious Humanists, more familiarly called "secularists," include many distinguished Americans who have significantly increased public awareness of the philosophy of Humanism. There are many books currently available that expound their position, but our present study must be limited to a survey of Ethical Humanism as a contemporary nontheistic religion. (For a fair-minded presentation of the varieties of Humanist thought from a secularist perspective, I recommend Corliss Lamont's widely respected book, *The Philosophy of Humanism.*)

A statement commonly used by the Ethical Culture societies to publicize their conception of Ethical Humanist religion declares:

> Ethical Culture is a humanistic religious and educational movement . . . working together to create a more humane society. Our faith is in the capacity and responsibility of human beings to act in their personal relationships and in the larger community to help create a better world. Our commitment is to the worth and dignity of the individual, and to treating each human being so as to bring out the best in him or her.

In describing the Ethical Humanist movement, this study is inevitably a personal interpretation. I have tried to be representative and balanced in my account, but some other member of the Ethical movement might just as truly speak from a different personal perspective. I am grateful for having had the privilege to serve as an Ethical leader (the movement's equivalent to minister) for twenty-eight years, and also for the experience of having served as president of the national body, the American Ethical Union. In the chapter that follows, I describe more fully these experiences and what they have taught me about Ethical Humanism.

During this past quarter-century, there has not been a society in the nation that I have not visited, not once but repeatedly. Ethical Humanist friends and associates are in every region of the United States. So are many friends and coworkers of the American Humanist Association, the Fellowship of Religious Humanists, the Society for Humanistic Judaism, and the churches and fellowships of the Unitarian Universalist Association, in which I began my life's work as a Humanist minister. To a limited extent, therefore, this book is a comparative overview of ethical and religious Humanism in North America. I also describe relationships with similar Humanist groups throughout the world, which whom I have enjoyed many valued personal associations.

I wish to acknowledge my gratitude to the American Ethical Union for encouraging the publication of this volume, especially to its president, Sophie Meyer, and to members of its publication committee, Arthur Dobrin, Jean Somerville Kotkin, and Joseph Chuman, who read the preliminary draft and made many valuable suggestions; and to my always helpful publisher, Frederick Ungar, and his staff. I am also grateful to Jack Tourin, former president of the American Ethical Union, who insisted that I write this study. To the late Joseph L. Blau, professor of philosophy and religion at Columbia University, who was a colleague on the Board of Leaders of the New York Society, I owe a special debt for his guidance of my effort to interpret Felix Adler's ethical philosophy. Unfortunately, Professor Blau's death intervened before I could share with him the completed manuscript.

CHAPTER ONE

The Greatest Idea in the World

66 The great use of a life is to spend it for something that outlasts it," wrote Bertrand Russell. Wise and thoughtful men and women in all ages have agreed that the greatest lives are those given to the well-being of others. In promoting human understanding and happiness, we discover our own deepest and most enduring values.

Many who belong to no church or sect—along with many who do—when asked to identify their creed, will reply simply: "My religion is the golden rule." Or they will answer: "Formal church doctrines and theologies are not important to me. The way in which I relate to others and to myself is all that finally matters." Without perhaps having a label for their faith, such people—to the degree that they live by these convictions—are practicing the essence of Humanist religion.

The religious philosophy known as Ethical Humanism (also called Ethical Culture) is a moral faith based on respect for the dignity and worth of human life. It is a practical, working religion devoted to ethical living, without imposing ritual obligations or prescribing beliefs about the supernatural. Thus it is purely a religion "of this world."

Yet this life-centered faith is not secular in the commonplace usage of being antireligious, nor is it to be understood as indifferent to religious values. On the contrary, for the Ethical Humanist, life itself is inherently religious in quality; to make this affirmation is simply to believe that human existence in this world is intrinsically worthy of reverence, that the world of ordinary experience is capable of inspiring profound feelings of spiritual devotion.

Commitment to the supreme worth (or sanctity) of human life is the core of the Ethical Humanist faith. This recognition of a spiritual obligation to treat human life *as sacred* persuades Humanists that their belief can, with justification, be considered as a religious faith.

In this connection we note that the words "sacred" and "sanctity" are derived from the same root as "sanctuary," meaning that which is set aside and sheltered as inviolable or holy. In other words, to treat a spiritual object as sacred is to regard it as "off limits," as not to suffer violation. The scope of religious history shows that the sacred object may be variously conceived. The sanctified subject may take the form of a god or divine personage, or find embodiment in a taboo or sacrament, or be revered as a mysterious power within a holy artifact. In more advanced stages of human thought, the object of faith may come to be conceived purely as an ideal value or a transcending moral or spiritual principle. Religious Humanism falls into this last category in terms of its object of reverence. To define the permissible range of religious veneration more narrowly would be unjustifiably restrictive and arbitrary.

Ethical Humanists contend that the dignity and moral worth of human personality should always be respected as the supreme end in view, the *summum bonum*, the supreme good to be observed. This affirmation of human worth is the starting point of Humanist religion.

Many Humanists, as religious naturalists, would go even further to assert in principle the sanctity of *all life*, even though the circumstances of existence may make it impossible for us to live without violating in some measure the existence of other creatures. But such violations should always be recognized as intrinsically evil. Like the Native American hunter who begs forgiveness of the quarry he kills for necessary food and clothing, we ought always to be humbled by the thought that life is infinitely precious and to be sheltered from avoidable harm.

Critics who accuse Humanists of being "man-centered" and of disregarding the larger world of nature speak in ignorance of the comprehensive philosophy that buttresses our moral and religious faith, a school of thought known in academic circles as Naturalistic Humanism. The restrictive and sometimes divisive label, "secular humanism" (which suggests that Humanists exclude religious values and ignore nature) only recently came into vogue as the special bogey of Humanism's fundamentalist critics. An artificially inflamed religious hysteria has been fanned by the less scrupulous Fundamentalist evangelists, who deliberately falsify Humanism's humanitarian ethics and social philosophy to portray the bogey of "a godless, Satanic religion" of lawless hedonism and self-indulgence.

But prior to the Fundamentalists' discovery of Humanism as a convenient bugbear for their attacks on secular science and culture, the term "secular humanism" was only rarely used in Humanist circles, as a review of the literature of the period will show. (The situation in Europe may have been different, where an organized Secularist movement has had a long and distinguished history.) In American thought, the time-honored and also preferred philosophical label that has enjoyed acceptance by both religious and nonreligious Humanists is the designation introduced above—"Naturalistic Humanism"—a terminology that denotes a conception of the natural universe free from supernaturalism.

As Naturalistic Humanists, we accept our place as children of an inconceivably vast and ever-creative universe. Whether individual Humanists, or particular groups of Humanists, prefer to consider Humanism as religious (the position taken here), or as solely philosophical, Humanists generally are in agreement that human life is the outcome of an incalculably dynamic natural universe in its ongoing evolutionary progression. In this conception of reality, there is no need to assume a supernatural intelligence presiding over the origin and destiny of life or the cosmos.

While millions of people in the United States, and millions more around the world, subscribe to the concepts and attitudes expressed above as a purely personal philosophy or faith, Ethical Humanism also exists as an organized religious and ethical movement. Founded more than a century ago in New York City as the Society for Ethical Culture, the movement has grown into a national federation of local societies known as the American Ethical Union. A European Ethical movement, headquartered in Switzerland, was organized soon after the American development.

Individual societies may be known as Ethical societies, Ethical Culture societies, or Ethical Humanist societies, according to local preference. But regardless of variations in name, all member groups of the American Ethical Union share the same essential moral and spiritual faith that has come to be known as Ethical Humanism.

Today Ethical Humanism is part of the global Humanist movement. In 1952 the American Ethical Union collaborated with the American Humanist Association and other Humanist and Ethical bodies in Britain, Western Europe, and India to organize a worldwide alliance of Ethical Culture and Humanist groups named the International Humanist and Ethical Union (IHEU). Although each member association retains its independence and historic identity, all are linked in a worldwide community for the promotion of Ethical Humanist principles and ideals. Some IHEU organizations, like the American Ethical Union, are structured as religious bodies in the inclusive meaning of religion described above. Others, reflecting quite different histories and interests, are purely secular (in the nonreligious application of that term). But all share the common denominator of loyalty to human values, respect for the dignity and rights of the individual, support for the scientific method and intellectual liberty, and commitment to a free, democratic society. All vigorously resist both secular and religious authoritarianism.

The Second Humanist Manifesto of 1973, a consensus statement signed by many leading Humanists, struck a balance between those holding religious and nonreligious conceptions of Humanism by acknowledging ethical religion as consistent with the Humanist philosophy, while rejecting autocratic and dogmatic religious formulations. In the opening paragraphs of the section entitled "Religion," the Manifesto declared:

> In the best sense, religion may inspire dedication to the highest ethical ideals. The cultivation of moral devotion and creative imagination is an expression of genuine "spiritual" experience and aspiration.
>
> We believe, however, that traditional dogmatic or authoritarian religions that place revelation, God, ritual, or creed above human needs and experience do a disservice to the human species. . . . As nontheists, we begin with humans, not God, nature not deity.

As the signers of the 1973 consensus viewed the matter, the valid and permanently valuable aspect of religion is expressed in creative idealism and humanistic ethics, not in unverifiable claims to possess secret keys to supernatural knowledge, or of assumed "revelations" that subordinate human learning and wisdom to twice-told tales of divine saviors and their pretended emissaries on earth. We must begin our quest for spiritual understanding on the basis of sharable human experience—the foundation of all genuine knowledge of the world—clearly observing the characteristics and limits of that experience. Only then can we even begin to address intelligently the conundrum of the existence and nature of God or "ultimate reality."

No matter how far our observations and discoveries extend from the presently understood cosmos into the unknown, our knowledge must remain always within the bounds of "nature"—that seemingly trackless cosmos of events, relationships, and processes in which we exist. This is what the relativity of knowledge consists of—the relational composition of all perceiving and knowing. The means by which we comprehend the world, organized within the logical structures of thinking and knowing, necessarily shapes our knowledge and sets limits to its reach.

Thus we can never penetrate "pure being," or know ultimate reality "under the aspect of eternity," to borrow Spinoza's telling phrase. An attitude akin to agnosticism is therefore fitting for those who face the human situation realistically and humbly in an ultimately unfathomable reality. But even within the limits of incomplete and fallible human understanding, we can live compassionate, meaningful lives of love and caring. The conviction that such a life is possible, with the determination to achieve it, is the cornerstone of the Ethical Humanist faith.

Discovering a Faith to Live By

Although the American Ethical Union and its member societies have a distinguished history of social service and intellectual achievement (as any reader can confirm by consulting standard encyclopedias), their comparatively small numbers make it inevitable that many people will never encounter an Ethical society or any other organized group of Humanists. The typical prospective member usually works out alone a personal religious philosophy and only then chances to discover that a spiritual fellowship serving these purposes already exists.

I can illustrate this best perhaps by relating my personal quest that led me to Ethical Humanism and eventually to a vocation of professional leadership in Ethical Culture. As a youth reared in a small Southern town of a typically conservative Protestant family, during adolescence I came to question the religious doctrines of my childhood training. What I had been taught to accept as infallibly revealed truth became untenable in the light of my growing awareness of modern scientific and philosophical thought. When I sought an explanation for these discrepancies, none was forthcoming. I was only admonished to "have faith."

In my effort to find satisfactory answers to my questions, I explored widely the field of religious history and philosophy. There was much that appealed to me in the life and faith of the Religious Society of Friends, the Quakers, especially in the spiritual freedom and universalism of their historically liberal "Hicksite" branch. But even the most progressive expressions of Quakerism still retained more of the traditional "religious" vocabulary and doctrine than I could wholeheartedly accept.

I discovered that the Unitarians and Universalists came even closer to my spiritual ideal with their rejection of orthodox Christian doctrine and their emphasis on a religion of character, reason, and practical philanthropy—beliefs that prefigured Humanism. But I knew that I was not a unitarian (note the lower case) in the historic dictionary definition: one who rejects the doctrine of the trinity and the deity of Christ, but who retains belief in a unitary (one) God. In truth I no longer believed in any kind of supernatural, personal deity, whether defined as the Christian trinity or simply as "God the creator." But my interest in the Unitarians revived when my dictionary—even then a well-worn copy as old as I was—gave me the surprising information that "the [Unitarian] denomination now includes in its ministry and membership a number of non-theistic humanists. See HUMANISM."

I pursued the reference to Humanism and learned that, among other meanings, it was defined as a religion "that substitutes faith in man for faith in God," (a definition that, despite its scholarly source, I recognized as oversimplified.) Still, I was assured that I was not alone in supposing it possible to have a religion without belief in a deity. The thought passed through my mind that some day I might become a Humanist minister.

Many questions still required answers. What would a religion without a doctrine of God teach? The answer necessarily pointed to ethics. So, with no available library books on the subject, I turned back to my large dictionary and carefully studied every entry on ethics. My attention quickened when I came upon the following:

> **ethical culture.** A religious movement that asserts the "supreme importance of the ethical factor in all relations of life," and avoids formal creeds or ritual. See AMERICAN ETHICAL UNION; SOCIETY FOR ETHICAL CULTURE.
> —Webster's New International Dictionary, Second Edition.

In college I pursued these leads and by researching the library discovered a magazine called *The Humanist,* edited by a Unitarian minister, Edwin H. Wilson, who also served as the director of the American Humanist Association. I corresponded with Dr. Wilson and later followed his footsteps into the Unitarian ministry, where I spent eight years in preparation and service. At about the same time that I encountered *The Humanist,* I chanced upon a copy of *The Standard,* then the official journal, now unfortunately discontinued, of the Ethical Culture movement. An inquiry to the headquarters of the American Ethical Union in New York brought me information and introductory books. In

Ethical Culture I found my religious ideals most fully and satisfyingly expressed. Even after I had entered the ministry as a Humanist Unitarian, I continued to look toward Ethical Culture as the flagship of religious Humanism. When the unexpected invitation came, I entered the professional leadership in 1959 as leader of the Ethical society in Washington, D.C.

For the following twenty-five years, Ethical leadership was my full-time vocation. That quarter-century was divided almost equally between my original post in Washington and a subsequent period of leadership at the New York Society for Ethical Culture—the society where the movement had begun a hundred years earlier. Indeed, in 1976, as Senior Leader in New York, I presided over the national centennial celebrations that inaugurated the Ethical Humanist movement's second century. During the course of my leadership, I was also privileged to serve a term as president of the national federation, the American Ethical Union. My friendships and associations extended to the international community as well, including involvement in world congresses (in both Europe and the U.S.) of the International Humanist and Ethical Union. During a trip around the world, I enjoyed the hospitality of Humanists in India.

Thus, this story of the Ethical Humanist movement—its faith, work, and philosophy—is a personal account told from the perspective of one who has known at first hand the life and heartbeat of this unique global community and faith.

With this extended association spanning three continents, imagine my astonishment to read in the press from time to time that Humanist religion does not exist. It is said to be merely a "myth" invented by extremists of the Fundamentalist right! Some of those who subscribe to this "explanation" grudgingly concede that a few attempts to organize Humanist congregations have been undertaken, but usually with the implication that such efforts have been unsuccessful or short-lived.

Yet if one counts the total number of Ethical Culture societies and fellowships and then adds the Unitarian Universalist churches and societies that are explicitly or predominately Humanist in orientation and practice, plus the various congregations of the Society for Humanistic Judaism—all existing examples of Humanist religious organization in the United States and Canada—the sum of such congregations would be in the hundreds. To that number must be added the members-at-large of the Fellowship of Religious Humanists and the considerable body of religious Humanists within the American Humanist Association, an "umbrella" organization that includes both the religious and the nonreligious. (In the case of the Unitarian Universalist churches and fellowships an exact estimate of numbers is not possible, since there exists a gradation from societies that are explicitly Humanist in orientation to those in which more traditional theistic views prevail.) So while the religion of Humanism in North America is small when compared to other religious movements, it can hardly be dismissed as a myth created by its enemies!

The Key to Personal Spiritual Development

Felix Adler, founder of the first Society for Ethical Culture and organizer of the American Ethical Union, believed that the nucleus of the spiritual life is to be found in the ethical relatedness of each person to others. It is because of our involvement in the lives of others that we are enabled to grow into moral and spiritual beings.

Adler expressed his insight in a deceptively simple maxim: "Act so as to encourage the best in others, and by so doing you will develop the best in yourself." This thought is what the term "ethical culture" was coined to suggest—the cultivation of ethical relationships on such a basis that the moral and spiritual potential of every member of the human community will be most fully activated. This conception of the moral life represents an ideal that we can and should strive to realize, but which, of course, we recognize can be only imperfectly achieved.

The flickering idea of the supremacy of ethics began to burst into flame for me from the moment of my search through the dictionary, seeking a name for a religion of pure moral idealism. What I discovered is far more than a name!

In Ethical Culture I found a Humanist movement consisting of local societies that serve in much the same way as other religious congregations—as humanly supportive spiritual communities—with the important difference that the "gospel" in an Ethical society is belief in the spiritual sufficiency of ethical living. Societies generally hold regular Sunday morning meetings—or assemble at such other times as they find suitable. They conduct Ethical Sunday Schools for children, sponsor worthy projects in their communities, organize adult education classes and forums, struggle for human rights and freedom of conscience, and unite with other faiths to promote world peace—in short, do everything possible that one would expect of a group dedicated to humanistic values.

The societies also provide pastoral services, conduct weddings, funerals, or memorial services, do personal counseling, and organize social and cultural events for adults and young people. Their professionally trained leaders serve a role fully comparable to that of rabbis and ministers and are authorized under federal and state statutes to function as ministers of religion—a right that has been duly sustained in the courts. In every sense of the word an Ethical Culture leader is a minister of Humanist religion.

A Religion Born of Human Experience

Humanists believe that religion has its foundation in human needs and sympathy and that religious knowledge is not different from any other kind of human knowledge. It is distinct only in the quality of the experience and the unique value that we attribute to the moral life. In brief, religion is a creation of human living, not a revelation from gods on high. As a result of their human origin and character, religious concepts are always variable and unfinished, requiring continuous correction and revision, if they are not to become obsolete and oppressive.

It is the *sufficiency* of ethics-being-lived as the foundation of an enriching moral and spiritual development that leads Ethical Humanists to stress its religious quality and potential. When the charter of the New York Society for Ethical Culture was amended in 1910, thirty-four years after its founding, Felix Adler urged that the statement of purpose clarify the religious character of the Society. The charter, thus amplified, states definitively Ethical Culture's specific concept of religion:

> Interpreting the word "religion" to mean fervent devotion to the highest moral ends, our Society is distinctly a religious body. But toward religion as a confession of faith in things superhuman the attitude of the Society is neutral. Neither acceptance or rejection of any theological doctrine disqualifies for membership.

The story of how this distinctive religious and educational movement came to be and how its philosophy was foreshadowed in the evolution of both Jewish and Christian ethics will be sketched in the next two chapters. But first it may be helpful to consider briefly two basic matters that may require further clarification: how ethical creativity becomes transformative in living and what exactly "nontheistic" religion means.

Moral Insight Grows from Living Relationships

Our sense of right and wrong emerges out of the process of living together as social beings. Humanity's social nature is the product of a long evolutionary development having its roots in the gregarious behavior of the species from which human beings descended. Yet in human beings the development of language and symbolic thought has given a whole new dimension of meaning to social feeling.

We do not, for example, merely grieve for our lost companions or offspring. Even other species exhibit feelings of pain and distress on losing their offspring or mates. But as human beings, we are capable of transforming our pain and grief into sentiments that provide solace and healing and that bring deeper insights into the meaning of life. Thus grief can take on qualitative meanings that have the capacity to heal and transform the character of life.

In the creative mind of a Sophocles or a Shakespeare, benumbing suffering can be transmuted into the rich colors of tragedy. The death of a Lincoln can recall a great democracy to its moral purpose. The martyrdom of a Martin Luther King may bring the shock of recognition necessary to arouse the moral consciousness of a nation and validate the dignity of all people. It may awaken in us, whether we are black or white, an awareness of our vulnerability as frail members of a human family subject to injury and suffering, exclusion and injustice. It may make us better people, better able to come to terms with our own mortality and enable us to live our brief lives with strengthened resolution, compassion, and appreciation.

We thus learn to accept our lives with serenity. Inner peace is the distilled essence of reflection on our profoundest experiences, separated from the illusion and superstition that unfortunately are so often associated with ideas of the spiritual. We come to recognize that the seed of the spiritual life is contained in moral passion. Spirit is born of flesh and nurtured in human love. We need not look to the occult and the other-worldly for the secret places of the inner life. It is the most delicate flower of human caring and love.

These reflections should suffice to illustrate the point that there is nothing of "mere morality" in the moral life as it is lived by sensitive and spiritually inspired human beings. Ethical religion is a *transforming* moral faith when it becomes vital—when it represents the harvest of first-hand living.

The Ethical Axiom

In founding the Ethical Culture movement, Felix Adler (in his time a widely influential philosopher and educator) worked out an approach to ethical living that he believed to be universally valid. He recognized that moral customs and ideas of right and wrong vary widely from person to person and from culture to culture. Nevertheless, he was convinced that a moral constant runs throughout the history of ethical religion and philosophy. That unvarying principle asserts that the individual human being is of infinite value and must not be degraded or abused. The most perceptive sages and teachers of all ages have accepted this rule, whatever might be the differences in their theological arguments.

In its usual form this "nonviolation ethic" is essentially negative. While it represents an advance over previous methods of regarding human beings, Adler considered it to be inadequate. He was dissatisfied with an ethical principle that fails to move from passive nonviolation to constructive moral engagement. He also considered the Golden Rule to be an inadequate guide to desirable conduct. "Do unto others as you would have them do unto you," leaves room for the temptation to remake others in our own image, to impose what we think is best for them. As

Bertrand Russell would later quip, do not do unto others what you would have them do unto you, because their tastes may be different!

Adler believed we can avoid the problem of projecting our personal moral egocentricity upon others—compelling them to conform to our expectations—by recognizing the unique personal difference of each and so to conduct ourselves as to encourage the fullest development of the special gifts and distinctive positive attributes of others. By living in this creative relationship, he believed, we would also actualize our own highest moral potential. He summarized this concept in the maxim that we have already cited and which is familiar to every member of the Ethical movement: "So act as to bring out the best in others, and thereby in yourself."

Of course, ethics did not begin with the founding of the Ethical movement. What Felix Adler and his early associates provided was the insight that the nurturing of ethics is primary in human development. As such it is a sufficient foundation for a life-giving religious faith.

Thus while the germ of ethical religion is at least as old as civilization—if we count the various religious traditions that have a strong ethical component—it nevertheless remained for the founders of Ethical Culture to make explicit the idea of ethics as the supreme principle and to build a movement on that sole foundation. But also many other men and women, including members of orthodox churches and synagogues, have valued their faiths primarily for their ethical and humanistic content.

Ethical Humanism stands in a tradition of cultural evolution that accepts all of human history and moral experience as part of its unfolding story. Unlike the established creeds that proclaim a completed gospel of salvation "once delivered to the saints," as the New Testament author of the Epistle of Jude has phrased it, Ethical religion embodies the ongoing living and learning of the human spirit through the ages. In his history of the Ethical movement, *Toward Common Ground,* Howard B. Radest observes:

> Some [religions] find their meaning in a unique event, an intrusion into history from outside sources. Others see themselves as set apart from their time in a sacred enclave. Still others root themselves in revelation. By contrast, Ethical Culture claims no revelation, no mysteriously touched central figure, no sacred mystery. It was not discontinuity that marked its birth, but a natural evolution.

A Different Way of Thinking About Religion

"Be ye lamps unto yourselves. Work out your own salvation," admonished the Buddha. Unlike the monotheistic prophets and reformers of Asia Minor—Isaiah, Jesus, and Mohammed—the introspective sage who founded the "Middle Way" that we know as Buddhism put no stock in gods and saviors. Like the ancient Roman poet Lucretius, Gautama the Buddha believed that if the gods exist, they are of no concern to us. If anything, speculations about the gods distract us from what we must do to accomplish our primary psychological and spiritual task of self-mastery. The early followers of Buddha, and even those today who are most faithful to his teachings, take great pains to prevent the elevation of their Master to the status of a divine being. Even the Buddha, superstitiously worshipped, would become a stumbling block to enlightenment.

"If you meet the Buddha on the highway, kill him," goes a somewhat startling Buddhist proverb. But the harsh maxim drives home a vital truth: No holy prophet, messiah, christ, avatar, or even a great god in heaven can do your spiritual or ethical task for you. Free yourself. Be a lamp unto your own salvation!

Although the more conservative students of comparative religion still refuse to accept early Buddhism as one of the world's religions (because of its lack of belief in a God), from the standpoint of this book—and that of many other students of religious philosophy—such an objection is unwarranted. To restrict religion solely to theism (belief in God) is the tendency of those who have never seriously considered alternate expressions of religious faith and experience. But religion is a term we choose to claim, and to apply to Humanism's spiritual life, believing that the function that religion serves in living remains as vital as ever.

It is natural, spontaneous, and inevitable to experience ethical commitment as religious, because ethical feeling functions as religion has always functioned, guiding and uplifting our hearts and minds as religion has always done. Ethical faith is unitive. It gives wholeness to personality and to our vision of life. Religion provides human beings with a sense of relatedness and rootage in the sources of our being, offering focus, direction, and motivation to our moral struggles and aspirations, undergirding social idealism, and highlighting the beauty and mystery of our universe.

Emerson was right in observing that we will worship "something," and we had therefore beware what gods we adore, lest they engrave their likenesses on our faces. If we serve unworthy masters, or make idols of false theologies and ideologies, we hasten to the destruction of our own designing. But if we desire to live and be free, we must plot our course by freedom's star.

What is Nontheistic Religion?

Since a nontheistic conception of religion is basic to Naturalistic Humanism, it may be helpful to be as specific as possible in our usage of that term. At the outset, it is essential to understand that "nontheistic" is not used as a synonym or euphemism for "atheistic." The atheist, like the theist, takes a definite position with respect to the doctrine that God exists. The atheist denies or disbelieves it.

The theist affirms it. But while the individual member of the Ethical Humanist movement may be an atheist, agnostic, theist, deist, or believe whatever else the individual regards to be probable or true about the God question, the Ethical philosophy takes no official position with respect to such belief. As nontheistic religion is defined, the prefix "non" should be understood to mean simply that the theistic reference does not apply. Ours is a religion or belief of a totally different type in which the God question is not of primary concern. As we have emphasized before, Ethical Humanism's starting point is ethics, not speculative theology.

Ethical Humanism is commitment to a way of life, to a creative relationship to others and thereby to ourselves, in which metaphysical and theological arguments are set aside. Whether or not God exists may be an interesting question. But the answer to that question—if answerable at all—should make no crucial difference in how we ought to live, how we ought to treat our fellow beings. My ethical obligations and potentialities—and yours—remain exactly the same, whether God exists or does not exist. Our shared task is to live decently, compassionately, and caringly in the world we inhabit.

Albert Einstein said it best on behalf of all Ethical Humanists when he commended the New York Society for Ethical Culture on the occasion of its seventy-fifth anniversary year. He noted that the idea of Ethical Culture embodied his personal conception of what is most valuable and enduring in religious idealism. Humanity requires such a belief to survive, Einstein argued. "Without 'ethical culture' there is no salvation for humanity," the great physicist and Humanist observed.

That thought, we are convinced, is the greatest idea in the world.

CHAPTER TWO

The Birth of Ethical Culture

On the fifteenth of May, 1876—a Sunday evening—a group of religiously minded freethinkers assembled for the first meeting of what was to become the New York Society for Ethical Culture, the first gathering of its kind anywhere in the world. To call this freethinking body "religiously minded" is to remember the special sense in which we previously quoted Einstein as defining pure religion. What Einstein identified as "a purely ethical conception of the religious life" was the inspired thought that moved the original little band in New York City to create Ethical Culture.

They could, of course, have organized their new society on a purely secular basis. Scientific rationalism and skepticism were in flower then, and the more iconoclastic spirits of the time were asking: "Why be religious in any sense? What use is it?" But the organizers of the fledgling Ethical movement understood the strength of religious idealism as a creative force in human life. What they still had to demonstrate was the possibility of constructing a religious society on the sole foundation of an ethical conception of faith.

The young man who brought them together had no

doubt about the possibility—and the desirability—of reconceiving religion in terms of ethical living. Indeed, he argued that ethics is the perpetually and universally vital element in the religious spirit. Everything else is local and circumstantial, destined to pass away as times and conditions change. But ethical relationships remain at the center of the social and spiritual evolution that makes us human.

The earnest speaker who addressed the gathering was the twenty-five-year-old son of Rabbi Samuel Adler, distinguished spiritual leader of New York City's most influential Reform Jewish congregation, Temple Emanu-El. Young Felix Adler—himself trained for the rabbinate, and until recently expected to follow in his father's footsteps—outlined his plan for a religious movement based on the unique principle of the supreme worth of the person.

The new society would be inclusive in its membership. It would be neither Jewish nor Christian. Felix Adler's goal was to establish spiritual community on the "common ground" of a shared concern for the quality of human relationships. The ethical faith that he and his supporters would build together would abandon the sectarian, theological, and ethnic divisions of the traditional religions. No ritual or ceremonial law, no scheme of supernatural salvation to dispute, no hair-splitting arguments about the existence and nature of God would be permitted to intrude upon a moral commitment to the fundamental dignity and worth of the person—a commitment suitable for the democratic consciousness coming to fruition on the American continent. A new people building a new civilization required a moral faith larger and more inclusive than the traditional creeds could accommodate.

None of Adler's ideas could be considered novel or original. What was original was the fervor of the youthful reformer and his insistence that the principles he announced should be acted upon. Already he was making a name for himself—and stirring up considerable denunciation from those who saw in his ideas a threat to the entrenched creeds. More adventurous spirits, recognizing his precociousness and charisma as a teacher and leader, praised him for taking the best insights of temple and church and employing them to raise religious and ethical consciousness to a new level of human community and service. The elements of ethical religion—of a spiritual humanism yet to assume definition—were already surfacing in progressive Judaism and liberal Christianity.

Under Emerson's inspiration, the Free Religious Association, organized at the close of the Civil War, had already proclaimed a creedless, open faith expressive of the inclusive spirit and humane principles that Adler now announced. But the FRA, which Adler had joined with high hopes, was proving to be a frail alliance of independent-thinking nonconformists. Their number included many of the most brilliant figures of the age, as well as some of the most idiosyncratic. They were led by bold dreamers and indefatigable talkers—all of which left the sober young rabbi impatient to organize a movement that would speculate less and labor more. It was therefore no accident that in announcing his Ethical Culture Society he declared its motto to be, "Deed, not creed." Later, recognizing that every way of life must link intelligent purpose to practice, Adler modified his slogan to read, "Deed *before* creed." Moral experience, tested in action, must precede and shape theory. Our "creed" evolves and gains clarity in the light of ethical living. Otherwise, thought hardens into stultifying dogma.

In formulating his ethical idealism, Adler never wavered in his conviction that active ethical involvement—the deed—must always come first. The prophetic conscience of his Hebrew heritage, which made good acts central to the spiritual life, never deserted him. Ethical Culture embodied the Hebrew idea of right living joined to the Greek humanist ideal of fearless, honest thinking. In that fusion of the heart and head, Ethical Humanism had its beginning.

While Adler's Ethical Culture had its roots in the moral and intellectual soil of ancient Israel and Greece, its immediate ancestry was to be found in American social idealism and religious liberalism. As noted above, Adler had joined the Emerson-inspired Free Religious Association before he was moved to create a separate and distinct "ethical culture." As critical as he might become of Free Religion's loose organization and endless speculative argumentativeness, Adler nevertheless remained a member for many years, actually serving for a time as president of the FRA. The Free Religionists provided him with his early teachers and role models—beginning with Emerson whom he visited in Concord shortly before the old sage died—and many of the young Adler's intellectual peers and associates.

The Free Religious circle included the "radical" or "advanced" figures from America's most freethinking denominations. They ranged from Lucretia Mott, a leading Quaker preacher of the liberal Hicksite branch of the Society of Friends (a figure destined to win lasting fame as a champion of women's suffrage), to Isaac Wise, yet to make a name for himself in the leadership of the Reform Jewish movement in America. But most of the FRA's leaders and rank-and-file members were dissident Unitarians, like Emerson himself who had never resigned his ministerial connection, despite his early departure from the parish ministry in Boston and his impatience with the temporizing of Unitarianism's New England establishment. Emerson recognized that the early Unitarians had taken a major step away from Christian orthodoxy, but he pressed insistently for his church to take the next logical step toward a "free religion" of pure ethics. Such a church could dispense with theology altogether, except insofar as every worshipper might discover first-hand the divinity within the self. It was an open and optimistic creed, generous in its estimate of human nature and full of hope for the human future.

Of greatest significance to Adler and his Ethical Culture adherents was Emerson's prophecy of the rise of a new conception of the religious community, which Emerson dubbed "the church of moral science." The new church would at first be lacking in color and tradition. But it would soon enough acquire warmth and beauty:

> The noblest literature of the world will be its Bible, love and labor its holy sacraments, Truth its supreme being—and instead of worshipping one savior, it will gladly build an alter in the heart for every one who has suffered for humanity.

For a young Jew, striving to found a universal ethical faith that would transcend the divisions that separated Jew from Christian, believer from skeptic, what could be more portentous than Emerson's coming "church of moral science"? But the name Emerson offered still smacked of Christianity. Adler's "society for ethical culture" was the obvious paraphrase into more inclusive language.

Jewish and Christian Liberalism Prepare the Ground

Before proceeding to recount further the story of Ethical Culture's origin and growth into a religious humanist movement, we should review the moral and philosophical ferment that prepared the way for its emergence. We can have no adequate understanding of the history and character of Ethical Humanism without tracing—and appreciating—the battles fought and victories won a century and a half ago in progressive German Jewish and liberal New England Protestant circles. If Felix Adler had never lived and the world had never heard of his Ethical Culture Society, it is reasonable to believe that something very similar to Adler's movement would have emerged as the likely fruition of ideas long carried in the womb of religious liberalism and free thought.

Reform Judaism and American Unitarianism are Ethical Culture's progenitors and remain its nearest spiritual relatives. Indeed, ethical religion under the name of Humanism has long existed as a well-recognized subgroup or tendency within the Unitarian Universalist churches (producing the American Humanist Association as its direct offspring). More recently the Society for Humanistic Judaism has emerged as a distinct branch of American Judaism. Both of these Humanist movements within liberal religion share with Ethical Culture a common philosophy—minor differences of emphasis notwithstanding—and a shared fellowship within the larger body of the International Humanist and Ethical Union, of which the American Ethical Union was a principal convener and charter member.

The Reform rabbis and Unitarian clergy of the first half of the nineteenth century were a remarkable lot. In intelligence, idealism, and moral courage the religious world has seldom produced their equal. They were children of the Enlightenment that had given the world the Declaration of Independence and the American Constitution, the French Revolution with its ideals of liberty, equality, and fraternity, and the impulse that had carried science and democracy to new heights. The liberal rabbis and clergy were also heirs to their distinctive religious heritages—ethical Judaism and a rationalistic form of liberal Christianity. Religion was a respected vocation among these two very different cultures that shared a similar regard for courageous scholarship, social conscience, and unyielding moral honesty. They were both religions of the free mind with a high regard for intellectual integrity as a spiritual virtue.

The Liberal Rebellion in New England Calvinism

The New England Unitarians, with their clergy in the lead, produced the first great flowering of American letters and social criticism—save for the fathers of the Revolution whose Enlightenment philosophy anticipated many of the ideas that the Unitarians made part of their religion. The liberal church contained a disproportionate share of the gifted men and women of New England who produced the poetry, fiction, essays, and political tracts that gave America a distinctive national character and humanizing mission. Unintentionally, their reforming zeal also helped bring about the Civil War through their abolitionist preachments. Through Ralph Waldo Emerson, who after graduation from Harvard began his career as a Unitarian minister, religious humanism has an ancestral link to the old established churches of the Puritans.

Although Emerson soon abandoned the parish life of Boston's Second Church for the more congenial environs of the lecture platform and the essayist's desk, he never resigned his Unitarian ordination and relished his role as a pundit and gadfly at various church convocations, such as ordination services for younger colleagues or an appearance as a commencement speaker at the Divinity School at Harvard.

From the time of the American Revolution a growing number of ministers in the parish churches in and around Boston had been suspected of holding unorthodox views about the nature of God and of departing from the strict Calvinist doctrine of salvation. Some were quite explicit in rejecting the deity of Christ and the trinitarian conception of God. Influenced by the rationalism of the Enlightenment philosophy, these members of the clergy had increasing doubts about Calvin's view of the salvation of the "elect." The notion that from the foundation of the world a just God had preordained salvation for only a select few—the elect—became difficult to accept. The "liberal" faction among the clergy reasoned that the doctrine made God into a monster and divine justice a mockery.

As rationalism and critical biblical scholarship became widespread, the progressives—already dubbed "unitarians" or "liberals"—began to argue that the doctrine of the deity of Christ lacked biblical foundation. It was not a Jewish but a Greek idea that had entered the primitive church through the speculative philosophy of the Neoplatonists and gnostics. Thus, the Trinity and the conception of Christ as a member of the Godhead was a pagan corruption—not an original and vital part of the Christian faith. To demonstrate their case, they found numerous scriptural references to Jesus's claim to be subordinate to God and his specific denial of personal moral perfection. Jesus had insisted that God alone was good, reproaching those who addressed him as good. Perhaps, after all, the old Hebrew conception of deity was correct. The Christian Church had engaged in nearly two thousand years of idolatry, elevating a human Jesus to the rank of deity. Biblical chapter and verse were cited in support of the liberal position. While later Unitarians would abandon belief in the authority of scripture and come to look upon the Bible as an imperfect product of human intelligence and faith, the first generation of Unitarians in New England endeavored to justify their position strictly on biblical grounds.

Another controversy developed over the doctrine of an everlasting hell. The more audacious found no clear biblical foundation for belief in unending punishment. Besides, the notion of torture without end debased the character of the deity. Some took a middle position, holding that the Bible seemed to teach that the wicked would be annihilated in the world to come. Others found biblical support for the doctrine, already being advanced by the fledgling Universalist denomination, that the reconciliation of God and humanity, achieved by the suffering of the Messiah, had redeemed the whole of the human race—an ancient doctrine that could be traced back to the early Church fathers.

"As by the offense of one," the apostle Paul had written in his great treatise to the Romans, "judgment came upon all men to condemnation, so by the righteousness of one the free gift came upon all men unto justification of life." As Universalists (and those Unitarians who shared their view) interpreted this and other Pauline passages, salvation was a process that would eventually be realized in all souls.

According to this view, God's mercy and forgiveness have already been assured. What remains is for erring men and women to recognize their destiny and forsake their unrighteous ways. The task of religion is therefore one of moral enlightenment and education. It was a short step to the view—which Emerson and the young radicals among the clergy soon took—to abandon the idea of Christ's messiahship altogether, regarding Jesus as purely a moral teacher and spiritual visionary with an exemplary conception of both deity and human nature.

While these concepts were still a long way from contemporary ideas of Ethical Humanism, the drift or trend of religious and ethical thinking is already clear enough. Religious doctrine is subject to the critical test of reason. And morality—or moral and spiritual growth—takes precedence over dogma or "revealed" truth as the essential core of the spiritual life.

The result of this ferment was to turn the old Puritan parishes of Massachusetts into hotbeds of reformist Enlightenment thinking. By 1806, even the old church of the Pilgrims at Plymouth had accepted a minister of Unitarian views, over the protests of an "orthodox" minority who were forced to withdraw and set up a separate congregation. Many tourists who visit the First Parish Church of Plymouth are unaware that it has been Unitarian for almost two centuries—and at least one of its recent ministers, the late Horace Bachelder, an avowed Humanist, associated with both the Ethical Culture movement and the American Humanist Association.

The result of the evolution of thought that continued among the Unitarian "radicals" up to the time of the Civil War was the emergence of a new type of religious philosophy. According to this view, ethics is the primary and most important element in religion. Character is the ultimate test of the worth or lack of worth of a particular faith. Good behavior is more to be prized than some pretended "orthodoxy" of creed. And while their view of the nature of God gave the early Unitarians their name—in spite of their objection to any theological label—it was their positive, optimistic view of human nature rather than any prescribed conception of deity that proved to be the decisive and guiding principle throughout their history as a religious movement.

Theodore Parker, one of Emerson's admirers among the Unitarian clergy and one who would gain a lasting place in American history as a militant and effective abolitionist, delivered a sermon in 1843 entitled, "The Transcient and Permanent in Christianity." Many who heard him concluded that Parker had proved that what was of permanent validity in Christianity was not uniquely Christian at all. What was transient, on the other hand, was the entire theological structure of the Christian faith, which Parker with incisive logic and historical erudition showed was an artifact of ancient metaphysics and myth that had lost its former credibility.

Unitarian progressives of the Emerson-Parker camp, who were often but not invariably identified with the "Transcendentalist" movement in New England, had reached a point where it became clear that their relation to Christianity was tenuous as best. Their logic pointed to the conclusion that Christianity can claim no higher degree of divine authority than can Judaism, Islam, or Brahmanism. At their best, each of these faiths contains the essential spirituality and ethical passion that we recognize in all the others. Each is to be admired as a unique voice of the spiritual life of humankind, differing in accent and emphasis, but one in a common affirmation of life.

Christianity had to surrender its presumptuous claim to be the "one true faith." Its airs of divine preferment were pure provincial arrogance—and ignorance. Emerson said so bluntly. On hearing a speaker assert the superiority of the Christian bible over all other religious literatures, the Concord sage, who delighted in the Hindu *Upanishads,* rose from his seat and exclaimed: "The gentleman only proves how narrowly he has read."

The "orthodox" Congregationalists now had a most welcome opportunity to taunt their more timid Unitarian brethren. For a generation the orthodox party within the Congregational churches of Massachusetts had infuriated the "liberals"—those coming to be known as Unitarians—by insisting that the Unitarians were not Christians. The respectable theologians and parishioners of Harvard and Beacon Hill had fired thousands of sermonic salvos to defend their Christian legitimacy. And now, the young radicals of their own camp were defiantly admitting the charge against them! Parker was ostracized from the fellowship of his more conservative colleagues, who refused to invite him to speak as a guest from their pulpits, as was the custom. But his congregants supported his heresy. In the absence of a centralized authority, each Congregational parish, whether "liberal" or "orthodox," governed its own affairs and supported the minister of its choosing. The very independence that had allowed the Unitarians to arise in the first place now made it impossible to check fresh departures from the traditional path.

Before it would end, the Unitarian denomination would come to include many congregations moving toward an explicit religion of nontheistic Humanism. That development, however, would not occur in strength until after

Parker, Emerson, and their generation had passed from the scene and the twentieth century had begun. But long before that date, Felix Adler would have begun his Society for Ethical Culture. And not surprisingly, Adler's two earliest professional colleagues as leaders of Ethical societies— Burns Weston in Philadelphia and William Mackintire Salter in Chicago—were drawn from the number of "radical" Unitarian ministers who were impatient with the slow, uneven evolution of their church toward a completely noncreedal religion of ethics. Ethical Culture answered their need. In years and decades to come many other ministers of the liberal church would be drawn into the ranks of the Ethical leadership.

Radical Reform among German Jewry

About the time New England Congregationalism was separating into two distinct denominations—the "orthodox" Congregational and the Unitarian—a somewhat parallel revolt took place in the synagogues of Germany, although nothing in Jewish orthodoxy was comparable to the grim Calvinist doctrine of eternal reprobation that drove the New England liberals into rebellion. Among the Jews of Germany and elsewhere in Northwestern Europe, the issues were cultural and ritualistic. They had to do with the question of how Jews viewed their Jewishness and of their place in the surrounding gentile world.

The times were changing. A more optimistic, cosmopolitan Jew, freed from the legally imposed segregation of the medieval ghetto, was emerging into the mainstream of European life. Behind the Jewish scholar, merchant, artist, and citizen was the longest and proudest continuous history of any people in the Western world. His accomplishment was the more remarkable as the work of a people who had lived most of their more than three-thousand-year history under foreign domination or in exile.

But, surely, the ages of the great persecutions were ending. Enlightened Jews and gentiles were both confident that this was so. The more civilized peoples coming into being—like the liberally minded and idealistic Germans who read Voltaire, Kant, and Geothe—would henceforth accept the Jew as neighbor and fellow citizen with equal rights and dignity. All that remained, it was supposed, was for the Jewish community to overcome the habits of former generations and breach the ghetto wall from their side too.

All the defensive strategies that had enabled a persecuted people to survive were coming to be regarded as outmoded. Christendom was changing, and the gentile nations were becoming increasingly secular and democratically minded. The Jew could be part of all this by choosing to update the customs and practices that had defined Jewishness. While anti-Jewish laws and prejudices still existed, and in some areas were particularly onerous, they steadily yielded to the progressive mood. Or so it was supposed.

Liberally minded Jews, who led in this spirit of optimism, were not naive or simple-minded. They responded to currents that ran deep in Western civilization, and the depth and violence of the countercurrents of ethnic chauvinism and anti-Semitism could not be foreseen. Still, the orthodox community doubted, and proposals to change immemorial traditions, sanctified as divinely established, separated the reformers from the more conservative and orthodox communities.

The reform-minded elements made a powerful moral and intellectual case. Even if Jews took certain risks—including the risk of assimilation into the non-Jewish population—they were nevertheless serving the historic ethical mission of Jewry to be a blessing to the nations. Theirs was the destiny of Abraham's heirs, which as the biblical prophets and sages had proclaimed was to bring their ancient teaching of justice and righteousness to the entire human race.

The essence of Judaism was ethical. Everything else was transient and dispensable. The Jewish reformers in Germany and the low countries were thus making the same point in their communities that Emerson, Parker, and their sympathizers were making in New England among the progressive wing of Unitarians. Ethics is the enduring and invaluable element in religious life. The ethics of the biblical tradition at its finest is a universal and humanistic teaching that affirms the kinship and moral equality of all peoples.

Was not Israel's loss of national independence humanity's gain? The scattering of the Jews among the nations was history's way—many would say God's design—to spread the prophetic teaching throughout the civilized world. As long ago as twenty-five hundred years, during the Babylonian captivity, the anonymous poet and sage known as "second-Isaiah" had dreamed that Israel, through its suffering as a conquered and dispersed people, would be the means for the gentile's eventual turn toward justice and peace.

This was a spiritually compelling conception. And upon this foundation Reform Judaism was built. David Einhorn, a principal architect of Reform theory as it developed in America, taught that the fall of Jerusalem had been a favorable circumstance. The crisis that Judaism faced in the nineteenth century was in a sense a second fall of Jerusalem—a breaking down of the walls that separated European and American Jews from their non-Jewish neighbors and fellow countrymen. Following the lead of his German teachers, Einhorn argued that the end of Israel as a separated nation had occasioned the rebirth of Judaism as an emancipated ethical religion with a universal destiny. The contradiction between ethnic particularism and ethical universalism had to be resolved in favor of a greater, more coherent good, the ultimate reconciliation of all people.

Like most other movements in their formative stages, early Reform Judaism, as it now emerged, was not disposed

to stop at half measures. It rapidly evolved into an uncompromising force to reorganize and refurbish Jewish practice
and community life in their entirety. The opposition that
the reformers encountered from the orthodox only stim-
ulated more far-reaching innovations.

When the phase of radical reform had subsided by the
latter half of the nineteenth century, Reform Judaism re-
treated into a more cautious, compromising stance. This
accommodation to tradition was nowhere more striking
than in the United States, when during the last years of
the century Jewish ranks were swelled by the rise of an
immigrant tide less disposed to discard time-honored
practices than were the original German Jewish pioneers.

The compromise producing the Reform movement that
has since existed represented sheer conservation of effort,
rather than a preplanned design. When Jews had been only
an aristocratic handful in Savannah, Charleston, New York,
Newport, and other early centers—born over many generations to the regional soil, speaking in the local accent,
and playing and studying from early childhood with
Quakers, Baptists, and Episcopalians, who had difficulty
enough figuring out what each other believed—Jewish
Americans became virtually another "sect," in a community
where all denominations were merely sects. Being Jewish
became primarily a matter of religion, without the imposed
"nationality" status that Jews in many other lands had to
accept.

Then, too, anti-Semitism was less predictable or certain
in America. While vicious in its many and often unexpected
outcroppings, it did not cause Jews uniformly to experience
exclusion and prejudice. For one thing, many of the sep-
aratist Protestant sects that had sought refuge in America
were philo-Semitic, like their Anabaptist progenitors in
Europe. Persecuted themselves, these nonconforming sects
held to a theology that on biblical grounds forbade them
to despise or persecute Jews. To be sure, they believed that

Israel would be converted to the messiahship of Jesus in the last days of the earth, but meanwhile Jews were to be harbored as God's chosen instrument for the salvation of the world. To harm a hair on a Jewish head was to excite God's vengeance against the persecutor.

Philo-Semitic and anti-Semitic strains have always collided in the American character—often in the same people, given the inconsistencies and ambivalences of human beings. But at least in America, Jews have always met a substantial segment of the gentile population motivated by acceptance and a conviction that they must be sheltered from their enemies. It was often not so in the countries of the Old World.

In this setting Jews moved quickly into the mainstream of American democratic life. Even in the conservative, antebellum South, Jews were sent by their states to the United States Senate. Florida's first senator was Jewish. And in the cabinet of the Confederacy, Judah P. Benjamin, a Jew who had ably represented Louisiana in the Senate, served consecutively as Secretary of War and State, and throughout the war was the most influencial adviser—indeed, the alter ego—of the Confederate president. At the same time, Lincoln called on a Jewish merchant and financier to save the Union from economic collapse. That distinguished patriot was Joseph Seligman, president of Temple Emanu-El in New York City, who was also to become the first president of the Society for Ethical Culture.

Seligman was only the most prominent of many religiously liberal Jews who have seen no inconsistency between their loyalty to Judaism and their membership in Ethical Culture. When the supremacy of ethics is understood as the essence of Judaism, as was emphasized in the early Reform movement, no inconsistency is possible. Ethical Culture, as Felix Adler insisted at the beginning of the Society's life, offers "a common ground" to all men and women of good will who unite to advance the ethical life. That ground is potentially universal in human experience. The task of Ethical Humanism is to make it an actuality.

The Judaism of the Future—Adler's First Sermon

Felix Adler gave only one sermon at Temple Emanu-El. The twenty-two-year-old chose as his subject the Judaism of the future—a theme that had the result of bringing about the creation of the Ethical Culture Society three years later. For while many, particularly the younger members of the temple congregation, were enthusiastic, more conservative persons of influence concluded that Felix was not a suitable candidate to succeed his father as rabbi. Reform Judaism was already under attack from the orthodox for dismantling the very practices that made Judaism distinctive, and the pillars of the congregation concluded that they did not need yet another voice saying the things Adler was proposing.

The title of his sermon bears attention. His subject was not the future of Judaism, but rather the Judaism of the future. A new Judaism would arise that would complete the long-continuing evolution from ritual to ethics, from ethnic or tribal loyalty to universalism.

The thesis itself was in complete harmony with the intent of the Reform movement in its earlier radical phase. While the congregants of 1873 were already slipping from their earlier militancy to a somewhat more comfortable compromise with tradition, they were still within living memory of the days when Reform had broken like a storm over the Jewish community, both in Germany and America.

The Reform movement thrived especially in Western European centers of intellectual ferment and diversity. Salo W. Baron, one of Judaism's authoritative modern scholars, has shown that Protestant cultures were generally favorable to the emergence of Reform, while the Orthodox and Conservative branches of Judaism were better adapted to the Roman Catholic and Christian Orthodox nations of Southern and Eastern Europe.

Reform offered a kind of protestantized synagogue—with simplification of ritual and with sermons and prayers in the language of the country rather than in Hebrew. Even the appointments of the Reform temple reminded visitors of Protestant churches. The organ, introduced early into Reform Jewish services in Germany, was anathema to the tradition minded, particularly to the orthodox Jews of Poland and Russia.

Other innovations were introduced as well. The orthodox Bar Mitzvah was modified to become a confirmation service for both boys and girls, in the manner of the churches. The abandonment of the segregated seating of the sexes, with women and girls admitted into the main portion of the temple for family seating, was a cause of controversy and scandal. Then came choirs, the introduction in many congregations of Sunday worship in place of the traditional Sabbath, the elimination of prayer shawls and other paraphenalia, and the practice of men sitting in services with uncovered heads. The rabbi began to assume the functions of a minister of the congregation.

But it was the change in the message that most distinguished Reform. Until twentieth-century anti-Semitism took an ominous turn, the Reform movement remained generally unsympathetic to efforts to colonize the Holy Land. Was not Zionism, asked the universalist-minded reformers, a retreat into outmoded nationalism? The future belonged to the Jew who would be at home wherever one's forbears had put down their roots, a citizen of the land of one's birth, and a Jew by religious conviction and cultural inheritance.

Saul Holdheim, one of the most audacious of German reform's champions, taught that religious faith and ethics should provide the sole standards of Jewish life. Folk traditions, nationalism, and the ceremonial law were obsolete.

Liberal Judaism, like the transcendentalist Unitarianism of Emerson and Parker, struggled to separate the permanent from the transcient in religious belief and practice—and the "permanent" foreshadowed the appearance of a religion of ethics to be known as Ethical Culture. But to fulfill that purpose Felix Adler would have to leave behind even the most emancipated of existing religions and create a new vessel for the new wine.

CHAPTER THREE

Ethical Idealists and Forerunners of Humanism

No one had a patent on the idea of a religion dedicated to ethics. Such an innovation was "a natural" for practical-minded Americans during the middle years of the nineteenth century. We have already recorded Emerson's prescient phrase, a "church of moral science," which he went on to say would be "at first cold and naked," a religion without the warming accouterments of the religious arts and ceremony. But, he predicted, "[It] will have heaven and earth for its beams and rafters, science for symbol and illustration; it will fast enough gather beauty, music, picture and poetry."

What went through the mind of Felix Adler as he dreamed of becoming the founder of such a visionary faith we can only speculate, but we know from Adler's history and early addresses that Emerson had cast a spell of spiritual imagination over the young philosopher that would remain vital throughout Adler's life and work—despite the fact that in future years he would come to prefer the moral and metaphysical system of the German philosopher, Immanuel Kant. He was convinced that Kant's philosophy of "ethical idealism," as refined by his later expositors, including Adler's teachers in the German universities (and as further modified by Adler himself), had solved the major problems of ethical thought, providing a firm and metaphysically correct foundation for moral philosophy. Nevertheless, the flame of spiritual passion that Emerson ignited in the young religious reformer never burned out.

By the time the American Civil War had ended, Reform Judaism and Unitarian Christianity appeared to have gone as far as they could go without breaking out of the boundaries of their respective traditions. The Reform movement approached the abyss and drew back. In contrast, by fits and starts and after protracted internal conflict, Unitarianism came gradually to incorporate nontheistic forms of ethical and humanistic religion. These newer departures from the ancestral Protestantism of the Unitarian church were explicitly—sometimes defiantly—universalistic, rather than Christian. This difference in the response of the two most liberal branches of Judaism and Christianity helps to explain why Humanistic Judaism eventually emerged as a separate movement (organized in our own lifetime), while Unitarian Humanism did not give rise to an independent denomination. For a time, however, as we have seen already in the case of Adler's early colleagues, Weston and Salter, Ethical Culture provided one of the few platforms where former Unitarian ministers of pronounced nontheistic views could continue to serve as religious leaders without mental reservation.

Emerson's transcendentalist doctrine, derived ultimately from Kant's metaphysics, but made lyrical by the nature mysticism of the British poet and philosopher, Samuel Taylor Coleridge, had become America's progressive creed. It was a creed that denied all creeds, containing a built-in fear of allowing itself to become a new orthodoxy.

In the Americanized version of transcendentalism as preached by Emerson and his New England circle, the teaching celebrated emancipation from traditional dogmas and rituals in favor of the immediate, original experience of divinity within oneself. The sacred resided in all things, if one had but the clarity of vision to see it. The Eternal One, made manifest as Nature itself, was fully present and alive within each specimen of creation. Especially within one's true Self—the Self that the sacred scriptures of the Hindu made identical with Brahman, Creator of the Worlds—each person could discover the inner God first-hand.

How much of this was literally believed, and how much was taken as poetic symbol for the unfathomable, inextinguishable potentiality of life and nature no doubt depended upon the temperament and intellectual subtlety of each advocate of the philosophy. This becomes evident when we consider that such disparate religious and philosophical movements as contemporary Ethical Culture, Unitarianism, religious humanism, pragmatism, New Thought and Christian Science—and other distinctly American schools of thought—are spiritual descendants of Emerson's version of transcendentalism. These offspring of a common ancestor may differ so radically that they would not easily recognize their kinship. Certainly Ethical Culture and Unitarian Humanism would see a close family resemblance in their religious philosophies and styles. But little likeness to the faith-healing, metaphysical teachings of Phineas P. Quimby, Mary Baker Eddy, or Charles and Myrtle Fillmore would be evident to anyone unversed in the geneology of ideas.

How could down-to-earth, commonsense philosophers like William James and John Dewey acknowledge their debt, and the indebtedness of American philosophy as a whole, to this poet-sage of Concord, Massachusetts, whose ideas so often skirt the boundaries of the other-worldly and the esoteric? Three possibilities suggest themselves. Emerson was either exceedingly vague in transmitting his ideas, or at least some of his admirers have appropriated his ideas in ways he never intended, or the ideas themselves are too abstruse and paradoxical to be reducible to a consistent philosophy.

Each of the three possibilities contains some measure of truth. Emerson was characteristically vague. He was a poet who rhapsodized where others merely parsed pedestrian prose. Hailing his greatness at the centennial celebration of his birth, Dewey explained that Emerson was a spiritual giant—a sage of uncommon sensibility—but not in the strict sense a philosopher. Emerson would have agreed and been flattered. To make a kind of fundamentalist doctrine of his free, spontaneous fantasia of God and nature would be to square the circle.

What remains vital for contemporary humanism in Emerson's influence is his insistence that each succeeding generation must discover the universe afresh, that old doctrines—the "revealed truths" of the ancestors—must not be allowed to blind our eyes to the outer and inner cosmos stretching before us. And, most of all, we should trust and strengthen our own powers of perception and insight. Emerson also respected science, especially its more speculative, intuitive hypotheses. His view of the world was radically evolutionary.

In the pre-Darwinian days of his formative period, he embraced the now-outmoded evolutionary ideas of Lamarck, which he found compatible with his doctrine of everlasting creativity and change, and with the cyclic progression of universes that he discovered in his treasured Upanishads. The ancient Brahmins of India, he argued, were much more far-seeing than the Judeo-Christian doctors of Western thought in grasping the everlasting wheel of creation. As a result of Emerson's influence, the impact of Darwin's theory of evolution posed little difficulty for liberal religion in America.

He also suggested a way of resolving the conflict between competitive individualism and harmony with nature and community that had bedeviled American life. Tirelessly he

insisted that we can be radically individualized, and at the
same time be joined in perfect union with the divine-human
and the cosmic everywhere. There is no contradiction. Individuality and community conjoin in each true self. The
personal and the social, properly understood, must proceed
from each other. The tragedy of industrialized, standard-
ized, mass civilization is that it has effaced the personal,
and in so doing has made the truly social impossible without
radical intellectual and spiritual change. Society must con-
sist of individual members, or it is not a society at all. Thus
he foresaw the tragedy of all revolutionary movements that
have submerged the individual in the collectivity.

It was an intoxicating, liberating doctrine of the free
personality harmonized with the social and natural environment. Yet it was a shrewd, practical teaching that sought
the radical recovery of the ideals of the American revolution. Those who accuse Emerson of having kept his head
in the clouds, of having ignored the problems of slavery,
economic injustice, and political corruption and oppression,
simply have not read him. Without comprehending his
meaning, they quote his own words against him, when he
wrote in his personal journal that he resisted the impulse
to become a social activist in order to stick to his calling.
But what they fail to grasp is that Emerson's calling was
directed by his social conscience and by obedience to his
vision of what life in the new age of American freedom
might and must be. He was dedicated to the propagation
of that vision of a better world, to be realized through active
faith in the human potential.

Emerson's early address, *The American Scholar,* was called
by Dr. Oliver Wendell Holmes "our Intellectual Declaration
of Independence." But Emerson's "declaration" contained
more, much more. It was an Americanized—and yet un-
compromisingly universalized—Sermon on the Mount for
a coming democratic dispensation. For those in his gen-

eration who listened, and they were many, Emerson's teaching seemed to be the clarion of a world made free of slavery, imperialism, and exploitation.

But although Emerson might be a born mystic with the air of a Hindu mahatma, he was also an incurable Yankee optimist who had lived through more than his share of personal tragedy and ill health. He remained always practical and ethical in his counsel. There was no running away from the evils of American industrial capitalism, or the slave system of the South, or the genocide being inflicted on the Native American peoples. For the serious student of Emerson there was no moral escape from duty.

Emerson had little use for the old language of theology and used it sparingly, and, when he did, always with a fresh construction. He made clear his distaste for Christian dogma. And his metaphors and images suggest that the realities of the spirit are not occult goblins, supermundane powers and taboos, or celestial demigods but rather the soul's own inner promptings, caresses of the heart, and spiritual hungers.

Despite his problems with Christian doctrine, the Puritan conscience radiates clearly in the emphatic moralism of Emerson's mind. Yet, his was a curious moral sensibility, especially for a New Englander descended from many generations of Calvinist divines. With a most un-Puritan-like temper, he never scolds or belittles, but with a sorcerer's voice calls forth the broken and discouraged to a perfected creation.

Ethics was the glory of human self-empowerment in Emerson's thought. While moralism had been an oppressive element in the Christian tradition, made even more intense by the Protestant and Puritan reforms, for Emerson our moral sense makes us free. Moral sensitivity enables us to become the architects and sculptors of an autonomous personhood. It was this thought that ethics can be creative and reconstructive that entranced the young Felix Adler and set him on the path that led to the development of Ethical Culture.

The Spiritual Stature of Felix Adler

Wherever we look in the annals of the Ethical movement, we confront evidence that Felix Adler was a resourceful and commanding figure. The movement became larger than the man, but it owes its distinctiveness to this founder who was extraordinarily gifted and energetic as thinker, educator, speaker, organizer, and religious exemplar.

In only one aspect of his work did he underperform— that is, for an intellectual of his ability and originality. He wrote little, except for the lecture platform. Most of his books, with the notable exception of *An Ethical Philosophy of Life*, written in his mid-sixties, were compiled from public addresses. Since modern philosophers are usually remembered on the basis of their scholarly tomes, Adler has not retained the reputation and influence that he achieved during his lifetime.

It is as an innovative educator, founder, and rector of the Ethical Culture Schools, that he is most widely remembered. Here he built largely on the foundations of transcendentalist and humanistic education that had been worked out by others, both in Europe and in New England, as we shall examine in a later chapter. Nevertheless, his adaptations from the experimental schools of others do not detract from his considerable accomplishment as an advocate and demonstrator of better, more humane, and effective methods of educating the young. And he gave to this child-centered teaching an emphasis of moral awareness and academic excellence that was distinctly his own.

What interests us now, however, is the philosophy of religion and ethics that Adler developed as the basis of the Ethical Culture societies. While earlier examples of ethics as a religion can be found in both Europe and the United States, Ethical Culture—the distinctive religious and educational movement bearing that name—was unmistakably of New York origin and of Felix Adler's design. It was not a matter of happenstance that Adler and his supporters devised a name that clearly distinguished their movement from the existing Free Religious Association to which Adler belonged and from which he borrowed so extensively. He reshaped whatever he touched to conform to his own conception of what the ethical ideal required. He was determined to build a unique religious movement.

It was to be a *movement,* not just an isolated congregation built around a single leader. Within a decade a small but dynamic constellation of societies had been organized—in New York, Philadelphia, Chicago, and St. Louis. Soon thereafter the four original societies banded together as the American Ethical Union, laying the base for an expanding federation of local societies.

By 1896, just twenty years after the beginning in New York, the Ethical movement had expanded sufficiently in Europe to inspire formation of the International Ethical Union, with headquarters in Zurich. The European movement prospered until Hitler's persecution of 1933–45 reduced the continental Ethical movement to a remnant of only one drastically diminished society in Vienna. Only in Britain was a trans-Atlantic Ethical movement unscathed by ideological terror and genocide. (As we shall see, the International Ethical Union was a direct ancestor of the International Humanist and Ethical Union and a link that spliced together the distinctively Ethical and Humanist strands of our common faith.)

Even after Adler had founded the Society for Ethical Culture on a basis that made it a potential rival of the Free Religious Association, the leaders of that organization in 1878 asked Adler (who was only twenty-seven at the time) to become their president, a position that he held until

1881. Despairing that the FRA would ever move forward to become the dynamic body that he had hoped it would be, Adler declined to serve further and turned his full energies to the development of the Ethical movement. Despite his disappointment with the Free Religionists, he remained a member of the FRA until it became inactive some three decades later.

Adler's continued affiliation with Free Religion is significant as evidence of his sympathy with the cause of a wider liberal religious movement. Although he was careful to preserve the independence and uniqueness of Ethical Culture, he did not break his ties with the fellowship of spiritual freethinkers who had pioneered the major themes of a faith based on moral feeling and natural piety rather than creed, scripture, and ecclesiastical authority.

That the Free Religious Association did not develop into a lasting denomination is often viewed as a failure. But it is equally arguable that the FRA finally dissolved because the controversies that made it necessary were laid to rest when the Unitarian association that provided most of its members—and apart from Adler, virtually all of its organizers and leaders—finally accepted its positions. By the close of the nineteenth century an accommodation had been reached between the more conservative Unitarian Christians of New England and the "Ethical Basis" group within the Western Unitarian Conference (then covering most of the United States west of the Atlantic seaboard), which made the FRA somewhat redundant.

The "Ethical Basis" bloc, as the term implies, were those, largely influenced by Emerson and the radicals of the FRA, who advocated a purely ethical basis for qualification as a member or minister in their churches and associations. They resisted all attempts to impose any theological requirement, however broadly such a test might be construed. Like Felix Adler's Ethical Culture, the Ethical Basis Unitarians regarded the dedicated ethical life to be inherently religious without any necessary underpinning of theological belief. This concurrence of views resulted in a close-working relationship between the leaders of the Ethical Societies of Chicago and St. Louis and their ministerial counterparts in the Western Unitarian Conference. There was even talk among Western Conference Unitarians of withdrawing from the Boston-oriented denomination and setting up an independent Ethical religious association to be merged with the Ethical Societies. Adler, wanting to chart his own course, discouraged his colleagues in St. Louis and Chicago from involvement in any initiative for re-alignment. In the East, where a more traditional Unitarianism held sway, relations with Ethical Culture were limited to those few ministers and congregations, such as Octavius B. Frothingham and his church in New York, who largely shared Adler's philosophy.

Within twenty years of the reconciliation between the traditional and more progressive forms of Unitarianism, religious Humanism made its appearance among the successors of the "Ethical Basis" Unitarians of the West. Although this development in another religious movement may seem to be far afield from the story of Ethical Culture, the event would hold great import for the Ethical movement in the twentieth century—both by confronting the movement with a dynamic and widespread rival for the loyalties of religious liberals and by providing a seedbed where organized religious Humanism, under that name, would first put down roots in American soil. These two factors have had immeasurable influence over the development of Ethical Humanism within the Ethical movement and in the wider Humanist world.

Meanwhile, the Ethical movement evolved its own distinctive religious identity. Nevertheless, even while emphasizing Ethical Culture as a religion in the sense of "fervent devotion to the highest moral ends," Adler was careful to add that membership should always remain open to the nonreligiously minded who might be drawn to Ethical Culture as simply ethical.

That inclusive attitude has been maintained by all Ethical societies and fellowships and is subscribed to by the national body, the American Ethical Union. Of all ideals on which the movement rests, the sole standard of ethical commitment, free from any other test or requirement, is the unifying constant. Even Humanism, the most influential philosophy in the movement, cannot be turned into an official creed or philosophy, except insofar as the humanistic spirit is conceived essentially to be commitment to human worth as the highest moral end.

Adler's Philosophy of Ethical Idealism

Among leading personalities of the Free Religious Association to whom Adler was directly indebted, Octavius Brooks Frothingham was foremost. The liberal clergyman who served as Adler's mentor was the son of a distinguished family of New England Unitarians and one of the most forceful and original of the Free Religionists. Adler also owed meeting his future bride, Helen Goldmark, to his association with Frothingham's congregation. For a time, according to his youngest daughter, Ruth, he was drawn to the idea of throwing in his lot with Frothingham's brand of Unitarianism. But as she recounted the family's recollection of the event, Adler's sense of Jewishness restrained him from joining an association with such close historical links to Christianity.

Adler's role model, as Frothingham certainly was (second only to Felix's rabbinical father), was a minister of wide reputation, admired by free spirits for his courage and intelligence and scorned for his "radicalism" by conservatives within his own denomination. A devoted abolitionist who had lived Theodore Parker's ideal of humanitarian universalism beyond the boundaries of Christian sectarianism,

Frothingham differed from Parker primarily in not sharing Parker's confident belief in a personal God and individual immortality. He found the basis of religion solely in humanity's spiritual nature and moral aspiration—beyond that, he believed, little could be asserted with confidence. His thinking necessarily tended in the direction of the ethical and the humanitarian. One of his books he entitled *The Religion of Humanity,* contesting the identification of that phrase with Auguste Comte's paternalistic and synthetic cult. (We shall explain more of the influence of Comte and his Religion of Humanity in the following chapter on Humanism.)

Frothingham argued that religion had always presumed to know more than lies within human comprehension. It was time for honesty and intellectual humility to replace certitude. Attempting to maintain some link with the theistic tradition, Frothingham—like so many others before and since—redefined God, conceiving deity as an impersonal unifying principle in nature that encompasses the ideal qualities, but not a sentient being who can be approached through prayer or sacrament. Only a life of service to worthy ends can bring human life into harmony with that "ideal being," as he called it.

This conception harmonized with Adler's developing thought of an ideal reality that is not personal or supernatural, but that transcends the secular realm as an objective eternal order. The divine—using that term as Adler sometimes used it—is fundamentally interpersonal and ethical rather than monotheistic and supernatural. Adler proposed to think of the divine nature not as a single monarch, but as a spiritual society of harmonious but completely individualized selves. Elaborating on Emerson's doctrine of divinity within every self, Adler conceived of the ethical ideal (which was yet real!) as a "Spiritual Manifold," a name designed to convey the idea of plurality in unity. Each unique being exists in transcendent spiritual community with all other equally unique beings. He cautioned that the pantheistic idea of a "World Spirit," such as Emerson's "Oversoul," should not be permitted to efface the separateness and distinctiveness of the person as pantheistic systems tend to do. In Adler's religious scale of values, personhood occupies first place. No theological or metaphysical principle that sacrifices the individual to the totality of being can be allowed.

In some of his writing of a later period, undertaken to establish the superiority of his formulation over that of Emerson and other Free Religionists, Adler was unfair in making the comparisons he drew. In his eagerness to establish the independence and uniqueness of his own system, he understated the emphasis on the particular and the individualistic that is so prominent in Emerson. In this Adler was not so different from many other philosophers, who have not always been generous in recognizing the extent of their debt to their first teachers.

Despite Adler's profound influence on the movement he had founded and led through its first fifty-six years, the Ethical movement never embraced as a central tenet his metaphysical conception of the Spiritual manifold—or "Ethical Manifold," as he sometimes dubbed it. Adler himself was determined not to bind Ethical Culture to any particular metaphysical concept or system, but to keep the movement open to a variety of approaches united on a common commitment to the supremacy of ethics. He thus set the example of distinguishing between his personal speculative philosophy and what he felt should be emphasized as the essential "common ground" of the movement. The example has been followed ever since. A particular leader or generation of leaders may expound, advocate, or plead, but cannot command adherence to a personal vision of truth.

For the sake of historic accuracy, as well as to understand today's Ethical movement, it is essential to record that Adler's transcendental idealism, with its mind-boggling "supersensible" divine community of ideal selves, rapidly lost ground following his death in 1933. Religious Humanism, grounded in the much more down-to-earth, pragmatic naturalism of twentieth-century America philosophy, largely displaced it within a decade.

The Lasting Influence of Ethical Idealism

What has come to be called Ethical Humanism (the viewpoint taken in this study) represents a meshing of contemporary humanist philosophy with the moral and spiritual insights of Adler's earlier philosophy of ethical idealism.

As previously noted, Adler derived his moral theory from the thought of Immanuel Kant, as expounded in somewhat modified form by Adler's "neo-Kantian" teachers at Heidelberg and Berlin during the early 1870s. Kant's logical rigor and clarity, Adler wrote in later life, appealed to his mature thinking much more than the looser Emersonian romanticism that had so strongly imbued his youthful idealism. Nevertheless, he was repelled by some aspects of Kant's moral doctrine (his justification of capital punishment, for example). And Adler was not convinced by Kant's arguments for belief in a personal God and the immortality of the soul.

What he held to be of transcendent value in Kant's system was the doctrine of moral freedom and the unconditional worth of each person. As promulgated by Kant and further developed in Adler's ethical philosophy, each individual must be esteemed as a unique and irreducible center of infinite value; each must be treated as an end and never be used only as a means. These concepts—moral freedom (with the correlative principle of moral responsibility) and the supreme worth of the person as the locus of ultimate value—have remained foremost in the faith and philosophy of the Ethical movement. They represent Kant's—and Adler's—lasting moral legacy to Ethical Humanism, despite the shift in philosophical thinking that became apparent in Ethical Culture after Adler passed from the scene.

The metaphysical and logical assumptions of Kant's idealism are so far removed from our contemporary commonsense views of the world (and equally removed from the logical-empirical conceptions of modern science and mathematics) that it is easy to understand why Kantian thought holds so little place in the present-day intellectual world. In addition to its difficult style, the validity of the Kantian system has been called into serious question as a result of the mathematical and logical analyses of philosophers of the past century, making relative and problematic the concepts that Kant believed to be beyond dispute.

An additional reason for the twentieth-century rise of naturalistic or pragmatic humanism is its compatibility with current ways of exploring reality—especially so because of its utility as the rationale of experimentalism and the scientific method. This relationship of humanistic naturalism (and pragmatism) to scientific thinking should become clearer as we examine Humanism more closely in the chapter to follow.

Nevertheless, despite the failure of his grand design, we should understand why Kant developed his philosophy and why it remains significant in the history of moral and religious thought. He believed that he had established a compelling case for the validity of certain religious and moral truths. While he did not succeed in proving his case to the extent he thought, he raised the level of ethical thinking to a higher conception of the human self.

CHAPTER FOUR

The Humanism of the Ethical Movement

The Humanist tradition is of ancient lineage. The term has been used particularly to designate (1) the rise of freethinking philosophy and science in ancient Greece and (2) the revival of Greek learning at the dawn of the modern era, known as the Renaissance, when intellectual interests turned away from preoccupation with Christian other-worldliness and once again focused on human values and pursuits.

In the context of this study, however, the term Humanism as a religious and/or secular philosophy of life is of more recent coinage and application. A term so widely used is bound to take on various shades of meaning. Thus, Humanism is sometimes used to identify a philosophy of life that entirely excludes the religious or that is hostile to religion. In contrast to this antireligious position, other uses of the term Humanism specifically embrace the religious as a valid and important aspect of human experience. But in contrast to traditional philosophies, religious Humanism conceives religion as having its origin and justification in human life and experience without supermundane revelation or sanction. It is this second position that is taken here. All Humanism, in the present context, is "secular" in its root meaning of pertaining to this world; but not all Humanism is *secularist* in that it excludes religious experience and values.

A pioneer thinker in developing a humanistic interpretation of religion was the German philosopher, Ludwig Feuerbach (1804–72). Rejecting the metaphysics of Hegel, Feuerbach embraced a form of philosophical naturalism, tending strongly toward a materialist conception of the universe, but retaining recognition of human consciousness as a distinct attribute of existence. Feuerbach's early writings constituted an attack on Christian supernaturalism, which he believed was no longer tenable in the light of modern understanding. Yet he extolled the principle of love and other ideal values as the enduring heart of religion.

Feuerbach is primarily of interest for his analysis of the idea of God or deity. His explanation became the basis of subsequent humanistic philosophies of religion. The idea of God, said Feuerbach, is a "projection" of human values and aspirations, experienced in consciousness as infinite in scope or value. Thus, a believer's God accurately depicts—like an image projected upon a screen—the innermost nature of the worshipper's moral and spiritual consciousness. Therefore, it is more accurate to say that God is conceived in the image of human consciousness than to contend that human beings are made in the image of God.

Feuerbach's most influential work on religion was published in German in 1841 and translated into English by George Eliot in 1853 under the title, *The Essence of Christianity*. Feuerbach denied that he was an atheist, although he did not believe that God exists except in human consciousness. Marx adopted Feuerbach's conception of religion as a product of human consciousness, but scorned the idealistic aspects of Feuerbach's philosophy. In fact he dismissed Feuerbach's Humanism as a halfway position between philosophical idealism and the uncompromising historical materialism and "class consciousness" that Marx advocated.

Marx contended that the need for religion would vanish when human suffering and alienation were overcome in a classless communist society. The Marxian thesis cast Feuerbach into the background for many European intellectuals who were inclined to believe that with human progress (whether Marxian or not) religion would fade away. But scornful of "utopian" ideas as Marx professed to be, he may have been a greater utopian than Feuerbach to suppose that any amount of social progress can ever relieve human beings of the awareness of their existential isolation and mortality. Most people have a deeply felt need to project meaning into their existences through a sense of spiritual linkage to a universe and an ongoing life process greater than their brief personal lives. It is this need that religious consciousness addresses. Because of the strength of this impulse in human life, all prophecies of the coming extinction of religion have proved to be in error. Perhaps, as Julian Huxley and many other religious Humanists have asserted and as Feuerbach suggested originally, an enduring human desire for self-transcendence is the vital and lasting source of religious sentiment.

Auguste Comte's "Religion of Humanity"

The first noteworthy attempt to formulate a complete system of religious faith and practice on Humanist foundations was advanced in France during the same period that Feuerbach was propounding in Germany his Humanist philosophy of religion.

Contemporary Humanists reject the artificial cast and rigidity of this pioneer system—and the domineering egotism of its proponent. We must nevertheless recognize the creative vision of the French philosopher of science and

founder of sociology, Auguste Comte, in conceiving what
he called "The Religion of Humanity." Comte proposed a
religion for the coming age of science that would reject all
traces of theological and "metaphysical" thinking, which
he dismissed as prescientific, in favor of a faith resting on
"positivistic" (scientific) premises.

Comte contended that human thought had progressed
through a three-stage evolution, which he designated as
the theological, the most primitive; the metaphysical, which
was the second or transitional stage; and finally the positivistic (in the sense of the natural or positive sciences). A
religion corresponding to the naturalistic (or the "positivistic" in Comtian terminology) would nurture the spiritual
feelings that Comte regarded as the permanently valid aspect of religious life. But in place of the worship of a supernatural god (corresponding to the primitive theological
stage of intellectual development), or devotion to a supermundane Ideal (the intermediate or metaphysical stage of
thought), the enlightened mind of the scientific era (the
third or "positivistic" phase of civilization) would take the
idea of a perfected and spiritualized Humanity as the object
of religious aspiration.

Comte did not propose to worship human beings, either
singly or collectively; he was well aware of human defi-
ciencies. What he proposed as the object of adoration was
an idealized conception of the ageless human pilgrimage
toward moral progress and fulfillment. Each worthily lived
human life, whether great or small, leaves some deposit of
value within the living spirit of humanity. Comte proposed
to envisage Humanity (he capitalized it) as a Great Being
(also capitalized) encompassing the living influence of all
past generations, reaching always toward the future
through the lives they inspire in the present. His was an
exalted vision of the unity and solidarity of all the generations of humanity, past, present, and future.

A student of Felix Adler's conception of the Spiritual

Manifold will be impressed by the striking similarities between Adler's ideal of a divine community of ethical persons and Comte's earlier concept of the Great Being of Humanity. (Adler, of course, firmly rejected Comte's naturalism and derived his conception from the metaphysical idealism of Immanuel Kant.) Neither Comte nor Adler found many among their successors who were persuaded by their proposals to reinstate the symbol of a divine being on a social foundation. Both post-Comtian Humanism and Ethical Culture remain stubbornly resistant to any overarching conception that might function as a God-substitute.

A major figure in mid-nineteenth century European philosophy and sociology—who coined the word "sociology" to designate his new science of society—Comte committed the blunder of trying to prescribe a complete ecclesiastical system. His plan included a fixed ritual and a hierarchical priesthood, which like Mary Baker Eddy's later blueprint for Christian Science left little freedom for development or innovation by those who followed. He had, for example, specified liturgical vestments and images of the saints of Humanity—who were to be selected and canonized from among the savants of science, philosophy, religion, and literature.

Comte's religious calendar was elaborately supplied with saints' days. The names that he chose for the months of the year provide a clue to his grand conception of history and philosophy. His proposed months were: Moses, Homer, Aristotle, Archimedes, Caesar, St. Paul, Charlemagne, Dante, Gutenberg, Shakespeare, Descarte, Frederic II (a Holy Roman Emperor who had clashed with the pope), and Bichat (a thirteenth month in the reformed calendar). No woman made the list of months, although St. Monica, Joan of Arc, Heloise, Mme. Roland, Mme. de Stael, and a few other had their saints' days. The miscellaneous pantheon included such assorted figures as Tasso, Milton, Spinoza, Schiller, and Bismarck. (Americans will be gratified

that Washington, Jefferson, and Madison were among the
Comtian saints.)

Most of Comte's humanistically minded contemporaries
dismissed the whole scheme as preposterous and an em-
barrassment to those who shared his basic philosophy of
science. Thomas Henry Huxley, celebrated as "Darwin's
bulldog" in the controversy over evolution, derisively dismissed Comte's religious scheme as "Catholicism without
Christianity." But despite his rejection of Comte's ambitious
design for religion in an age of science, Huxley lectured
on ethics from an evolutionary perspective and anticipated
the rise of a religious faith responsive to the findings and
methods of science (an undertaking that his grandson, Sir
Julian Huxley, would develop in the twentieth century.)

T. H. Huxley spoke for most of his contemporaries, especially in the English-speaking world, in rejecting Comte's
"Positive Religion" as contrary to the open, libertarian
temper of science. Nevertheless, Comte's philosophy enjoyed a measure of success in Europe and became a significant intellectual movement in South America, especially
in Brazil, where positivist temples were established and
prospered.

In London a positivist temple was founded by English
followers of Comte, who quietly dropped the more ex-
travagant features of his system. The London group attracted a small but distinguished circle of devotees, including Frederic Harrison, who lectured widely in Britain
and the United States on Comte's philosophy, the ethics
of democracy, and humanitarian idealism. Harrison admired the American contribution to democratic thought
and social idealism. At a time when it was not popular in
Britain to extol the merits of American ideas and institutions, he became an enthusiastic champion of the distinctive
civilization arising in the United States. Highly regarded
for the quality of his personal character by many who did

not share his enthusiasm for Comte's ideas, Harrison did much to prepare the ground for a distinctively Humanist philosophy of religion (albeit not Comte's system) in Britain and the United States.

The London circle of Comtists popularized the term "Humanism" (in the religious sense) for the English-speaking world, a contraction of "The Religion of Humanity," which many religiously minded freethinkers were appropriating for their own usage. As mentioned before, Felix Adler's mentor in the Free Religious Association, Octavius B. Frothingham, was one of those who borrowed Comte's terminology for his own version of liberal religion. In his book, *The Religion of Humanity*, Frothingham protested that the phrase was too precious to be monopolized by Comte's eccentric formulation. As with the Religion of Humanity, so with its derivative, Humanism! Much ink continues to flow over the question of who has a rightful claim to a term so obviously appealing.

The American Ethical movement, while always Humanist in the broad sense, avoided the use of the term during Adler's lifetime, in large measure because the founder of Ethical Culture feared that such commonly shared terminology would confuse his distinctive ethical philosophy with other schools of thought which he regarded as flawed. But after Adler passed from the scene, the view prevailed that the range of beliefs among Ethical Culturists is as wide as the variety existing among other religious and secular Humanists.

Compared to the broad areas of agreement and the common stock of ideas that are shared by all Humanist groups and associations, the differences are minor. As a frequently voiced comparison expresses it: Ethical Culture is a particular historic movement within the larger tradition of Humanism, with its own approach and emphasis, in much the same way that Methodism is a distinctive body within Christianity. Ethical Humanism identifies the Ethical movement's special character and place within the larger world of Humanism.

Religious Humanism in the Twentieth Century

Auguste Comte died in 1857. His proposal for the Religion of Humanity was the work of his final years, the keystone in the arch of a comprehensive system of positive philosophy. With rejection of his elaborate architecture for Positive Religion, the task of constructing a Humanist philosophy of religion fell to others, and only gradually emerged from the scientific and ethical controversies of the latter half of the nineteenth century. As a coherent and distinctive philosophy of religion and ethics, Humanism is largely a development of the present century. Its eclectic character, the product of many divergent points of view, requires repeated emphasis.

When the term Humanism came to be applied to an organized religious trend within the liberal churches in North America, the label was directly borrowed from its Comtian source. John H. Dietrich, who had recently transferred from the Dutch Reform ministry to Unitarianism. About 1913, he began using "Humanism" to identify his non-theistic philosophy of religion to his Spokane, Washington, congregation. (Later he moved to the Unitarian Society of Minneapolis, where during a thirty-year ministry he established a citadel of religious Humanism that has remained strong to the present day.) He soon discovered that another Unitarian minister, Curtis W. Reese, was preaching the same naturalistic interpretation under the somewhat cumbersome term, "The Religion of Democracy." (Reese, who later served for many years as Director of the Abraham Lincoln Center in Chicago, a settlement house with extensive social and educational services for the poor, always articulated a keen social conscience and a profound com-

mitment to democracy as a moral and spiritual concept.)
Reese and Dietrich conferred at a denominational conference and Reese agreed that "Humanism" was the more
satisfactory term for the far-reaching reconstruction of religion that he and Dietrich were propounding.

Dietrich, dubbed "the father of religious Humanism" by
a widely used encyclopedia of religion, later wrote that he
first encountered the term as a religious designation in the
text of a lecture delivered to the London Ethical Society
by an advocate of Comte's philosophy. (The Ethical Union
in Britain had described their movement as Humanist by
the turn of the century—, that is, more than a decade before Dietrich took up the idea in America.) Thus, while
religious Humanism in America originally took root in the
congregations of the "Ethical Basis" Unitarians of the West,
gaining general acceptance in the American Ethical movement only after Adler's death in 1933, the Ethical Union
in Britain had earlier served as a seedbed for spreading
the philosophy beyond its original Comtian limits. But little
remained of Comte's elaborate "Religion of Humanity"
except agreement on the human origin and focus of religion and the acceptance of a naturalistic (nonsupernat-
uralist) world-view.

The Ethical Leaders' 1965 Statement Defining Ethical Humanism

In 1965 the National Leaders Council (then called the
Fraternity of Leaders) reviewed the question of the Ethical
movement's identification with Humanism and formally
adopted a position paper prepared by a special commission
on philosophy chaired by the late Joseph L. Blau. While
not offered as a creed binding on individual members or
leaders, the declaration represented a consensus of the
Ethical leadership on the relationship of the movement to
the Humanist faith and philosophy and to the world Hu-

manist movement. (The leaders' statement was later published among the documents of the World Congress of the International Humanist and Ethical Union, meeting in Paris in the summer of 1966.)

The statement had two principal purposes: (1) To define Humanism as the term that had come to be used in the Ethical movement during the previous thirty years, and (2) to interpret the relationship of Ethical Culture to the more general Humanist community and its perspective. I served as a member of the Blau commission and drafted the text upon which the leaders' discussion and final statement were based. Because the statement addresses questions considered in the present chapter, it is perhaps useful to quote its most pertinent sections (edited only to conform to present gender usage). While the document is limited in its scope to a basic affirmation of Ethical Culture as a distinctive form of Humanism, it remains instructive as it describes the commonly agreed basis for our Humanist identity, as the leaders' council viewed the matter a quarter of a century ago. The slightly abridged statement follows:

Ethical Culture as a Humanist Movement

Ethical Culture is a Humanist movement. Even before [it] came to be described as such, we were a Humanist movement in our essential purposes and values, the first [such movement] of national and international scope to develop an ethical, social and religious philosophy on a non-creedal, non-theistic basis. This foundation has been sufficiently broad and flexible to accommodate a variety of philosophical approaches.

From the beginning, our founders, leaders and innumerable workers have been Humanists in their social vision and practical labors and their stress upon human capacities and dignity. They have been Humanists in placing our human relationship to our fellow beings and the human community at the center of their moral and spiritual quest. They have been Humanists in believing that human beings must assume responsibility for the direction of human life and destiny. For nearly a century this common ground has united us without restricting our freedom to explore or to hold a variety of philosophical and metaphysical positions. We have held to the maxim: "Diversity in the creed; unity in the deed."

In the context of ethical and religious philosophy, and as a way of life which many men and women are coming to accept as an alternative to the supernaturalist and other-worldly religions, Humanism is a tradition which runs with increasing force through the thought and life of civilization. No group or association can lay claim to a monopoly on the name or the tradition; to attempt this would be an expression of exclusiveness and sectarianism contrary to the spirit and character of Humanism itself.

Thus, in identifying ourselves as Humanist, we affirm our participation in a great and living heritage, the common property of all who value freedom, who affirm this life and this world, who cherish the life of reason and the scientific method, and who seek, within the framework of the human enterprise—relying upon natural and human resources—to create the good society and to uphold the dignity and worth of the person.

But only insofar as the name Humanist is preserved from restrictive and dogmatic usages do we apply it to ourselves. Ethical Culture, dedicated as it is without reservation to the worth of the person, and moved by a spirit akin to reverence in its search to understand the deep resources of human life and nature, cannot lend itself to creed-like doctrinalism, whether that tendency appears in religious, secular or political dress. In our movement, "Humanist" means a broadly defined and commonly held commitment and faith, not a particular philosophical or metaphysical style. Neither does it signify among us a particular emphasis or position with respect to either the religious or the secular aspects of our philosophy.

We reaffirm the term Ethical Humanist, adopted officially in the language of the Declaration of the Amsterdam Congress, which in 1952 established the International Hu-

manist and Ethical Union. We find "Ethical Humanist" to
be a designation that appropriately recognizes distinctive
organizational histories and traditions, at the same time
confirming a shared and corporate endeavor as a united
world movement.

As several of the older leaders remarked at the time,
adoption of the position paper by consensus represented
a philosophical watershed in Ethical Culture. To be sure
the content of the declaration was not new. With only a
few reservations, Humanism conceived in the spirit described had constituted the message and prevailing vocabulary of Ethical Culture in America for more than a generation. (In Britain, the leaders of the Ethical Union had
issued a statement at the beginning of the twentieth century
that conceived the Ethical movement as Humanist.)

What the Blau commission achieved was recognition that
Ethical Culture (or Ethical Humanism, as many were coming to designate the movement) is an integral part of contemporary world Humanism, but it also stipulates that our
underlying Humanist premise does not compromise our
commitment to intellectual diversity. Humanism is an attitude, an orientation, and a way of approaching moral and
religious questions, but it is not a closed system or orthodoxy. To become such would deprive it of the rational and
scientific temper that has guided the ageless ethical and
spiritual quest of Humanists.

At the same time, we faced the fact that there are as
many conflicting ethical doctrines in the world as there are
fractious theologies or religious creeds. In their early optimism, the founders of Ethical Culture and their philosophical forerunners failed to anticipate how fragmented
and disputed ethical theory would become in the twentieth
century. The issues that Immanuel Kant and his school of
ethical idealism thought they had solved have proved to

be far from settled. Ethical theory is as controversial as theological and metaphysical theory. Ethical Humanists cannot presume to transcend the battle. We have our own case to make on our own grounds.

While we cannot expect to be any more successful than our predecessors in providing "definitive" or "self-evident" answers—if indeed such answers were possible—we should at least attempt to be reasonably clear about our deepest moral and spiritual values and recognize their foundations in thought. We find our ethical values imbedded in the attitudes of mind and heart that have constituted the enduring tradition of Humanism, a moral and intellectual tradition at least as ancient as Greek thought and the great world religions. The highest and most enduring values of that tradition are integrally related to respect for freedom of the mind and the principled search for truth.

As a member of the commission on philosophy, I addressed these considerations in a background paper prepared for discussion by the leaders' council. I argued that "ethics in general" is no more possible as a neutral ground for transcending the world's conflicting ideologies than is religion in general. We may assert a universalist view of the human family affirming the moral dignity and rights of all people, but a racist or a national chauvinist will not accept our assumptions. This is precisely the dispute that separates humanistic ethics from contrary value systems. I argued:

But if there is no "ethics" in general, just as there is no "God" in general as a meaningful term, we must determine *what our ethic is* among the conglomeration of competing ethics. To my mind our distinctive ethic is and always has been a humanistic ethic, given definition by the liberal, humanitarian heritage from which it has emerged. As such it stands forth as a rival to those ethics that rest upon authoritarian, other-worldly or other non-humanistic bases. Felix Adler acknowledged as much when he made his transcendentalist philosophy optional for Ethical Culture, but at the same time affirmed the worth of the person as the essential ground.

The nature of this specific ethic indicates our place in the Humanist world and at the same time defines our essentially religious character—with the object of the religious sentiment radically reconstructed. I would argue that our ethic and our religious nature are indivisible and symbiotic. We are not an ethical movement which has secondarily embroidered a religious frill. We were religious in the logic of our ethic even before we were fully conscious of the religious implications. Ours is fundamentally an ethic of reverence for life and for its creative vision.

I quote this paper at some length to illustrate the range of issues under discussion. While not every leader shared my emphasis on the essential convergence of the ethical and the religious aspects of our Ethical faith, all agreed completely that the contemporary world has shown only too vividly the breakdown of any unifying ethical consensus, making it urgent for us to recognize the sharp cleavage between humanistic ethical philosophies and those systems that denigrate human nature in favor of dogmatic, authoritarian ideologies.

We agreed that our position represented an evolution and a fruition of the ethical postulate (human worth) upon which Felix Adler had founded Ethical Culture. Ethical Humanism is simply the flowering of that principle in terms of twentieth-century experience under the impact of the conceptual revolutions in science and philosophy. After extended discussion over several sessions, I was authorized by the leaders' council to put in final form the statement quoted above, which thereby became the public position of the leadership on the Humanist character of the Ethical movement.

Humanism Becomes a Major Philosophical Current

Ethical and religious Humanism might have remained little known currents within two numerically small religious groupings, Ethical Culture and Unitarianism (with a lesser impact on the closely related Universalist denomination), except for the adoption of their viewpoint by an influential body of scientists, philosophers, and journalists. In the short period between 1927 and 1937 a torrent of books, articles, sermons, and lectures poured forth to establish Humanism as what one Christian polemicist described as "the next battle line."

The first major fusillade of this Humanist advance was fired by the biologist grandson of Darwin's old champion. Like his illustrious grandfather, Julian Huxley acquired an early reputation as a religious nonconformist. (Julian recalled that when as a young man he was invited to represent the Huxley family at a long-overdue occasion to memorialize the late T. H. Huxley's scientific contributions, the king declined to participate as he normally did, expressing disapproval of the elder Huxley's agnosticism. Yet, many years later Julian would be knighted.)

If Julian Huxley's Humanism provoked Christian theologians to do battle, that certainly was not in the spirit of his book, *Religion Without Revelation,* published in December, 1927. Huxley's intent was to provide an intellectual foundation for his deeply felt religious consciousness. Admitting that he rejected the whole of Christian doctrine and had no belief in a supernatural God, he nevertheless experienced a profoundly religious feeling for the world of nature and for life itself. These feelings, he contended, were distinctly religious in tone and clearly distinguishable from the aesthetic love of music, poetry, and great art that so often accompany religious emotion. Huxley argued that to understand the human and natural origin of this experience is by no means to explain it away. To believe otherwise is as absurd as to suppose that we have discredited feelings of sexual attraction and love simply because we can explain their biochemical basis.

Huxley discovered in his own consciousness that religious sentiment and appreciation provide human life with its most valuable and enduring qualities and that this quality of experience is entirely independent of any theological or metaphysical supposition. Religious experience springs from our natural capacities as human beings. (We shall examine more closely Huxley's description of a rich inner life in the following chapter on spiritual values in religious Humanism.)

Huxley's *Religion Without Revelation*, which sold widely and was twice revised and reprinted during his lifetime, was almost immediately followed in the United States by a stream of similar books by leading philosophers and journalists. Within the year Roy Wood Sellars, a philosopher at the University of Michigan, published *Religion Comes of Age*, advocating naturalistic humanism. In 1929 the young Walter Lippmann, already a celebrity as journalist and social critic, wrote the best-selling *A Preface to Morals*. His book has won a permanent place in the literature of humanistic ethics and is especially valuable in refuting the absurd but widely believed charge that Humanism teaches short-term hedonism and moral nihilism. "If it feels good, do it," may be a fundamentalist extremist's grotesquery of Humanist ethics; but any fair-minded reader of Lippmann's conception of the moral life will be impressed by the balance, thoughtfulness, and spiritual maturity of a sensitive Humanist ethicist.

During the same year (1929), Edward Scribner Ames's book, *Religion*, and Henry Nelson Wieman's *The Wrestle of Religion with Truth* set forth widely discussed concepts of religious naturalism. Both Ames and Wieman were associated with the circle of intellectually progressive philosophers of democracy at the University of Chicago. Charles

Francis Potter, a popular clergyman and Humanist lecturer in New York, wrote *Humanism, A New Religion* in 1930.

In 1933, Professor J. A. C. F. Auer of the Harvard Divinity School, produced *Humanism States Its Case;* and the following year saw the publication of John Dewey's *A Common Faith,* developed from the Terry Lectures that he had recently delivered at Yale University. This small volume, setting forth the religious views of America's foremost living philosopher—many would say the greatest in our national history—would alone have assured public notice for religious Humanism. Finally, the great decade of Humanist books closed in 1937 with publication of *Man's Search for the Good Life,* by A. Eustace Haydon, professor of religion at the University of Chicago and future leader of the Chicago Ethical Society.

The Humanist Manifesto of 1933: A Religious Platform

The year before John Dewey issued *A Common Faith* he had put his signature to a document that summarized the theses that he and the thirty-three other signers considered to be the major propositions of religious Humanism. The Humanist Manifesto was never intended to be a creed or to be a final and definitive statement of Humanist belief. Almost every Humanist will have reservations about one point or another. The Manifesto represented only a consensus of a particular group of signers at a specific moment in history. Nevertheless the document became—and remains—the most widely known and representative expression of the Humanist movement as it emerged during the first third of the twentieth century.

Although it is sometimes asserted that a subsequent document issued forty years later, titled Humanist Manifesto II, "supersedes" the original statement, such a presumption is absurd. The work of the original group stands on its

own authority, and since the document claimed to represent only a particular group of signers, it is beyond anyone's
power to revise their historic consensus now. (The present
writer served as an American Ethical Union representative
on the Executive Committee of *The Humanist* magazine that
in 1973 prepared and issued Humanist Manifesto II. It
was never suggested that we were canceling the work of
our distinguished predesessors, most of whom were no
longer alive. We simply applied the same essential spirit to
the issues of our time.) This point is worth keeping in mind
as we review a variety of group statements in Humanist
history. Our purpose is not to shape a final and definitive
doctrine—an undertaking that would be inconsistent with
the free-thought principle upon which Humanism is
based—but to understand the themes and general perspective that have shaped the movement's character and
development. It should be noted that some of the most
thoughtful Humanist leaders declined to sign either document, because of their specific reservations or from opposition to any statement that might suggest a creed.

Of the thirty-four signers of the original Humanist
Manifesto, exactly one-half were clergy: Fifteen Unitarian
ministers, one Universalist (the two denominations had not
yet merged), and one Reform rabbi. Most of the other sev-
enteen signers were philosophers or educators, including
the Director of the Ethical Culture Schools of New York,
V. T. Thayer. Thayer was later elected to membership in
the Fraternity of Leaders (National Leaders Council) of
the American Ethical Union. Two other signers, Professor
A. Eustace Haydon and Lester Mondale, then a Unitarian
minister, were subsequently to serve as Ethical leaders.

Of the academics who signed, several were members of
churches of the predominately humanistic Western Unitarian Conference. Altogether a sizable majority of the
signers were affiliated with Unitarian Humanism, liberal
Judaism, or the Ethical Culture movement. Only two or

three are known to have held strong nonreligious (secularist) views—and even they, for whatever reasons, agreed to affix their names to a document that strongly asserted the religious character of Humanism. This is important to consider in the present intellectual climate that, thanks largely to fundamentalist propaganda, erroneously equates Humanism, and particularly the Humanist Manifesto, with an antireligious position.

Key sentences of the Manifesto advert to issues that remain contested today in religious controversy. The preamble of the Manifesto sets forth a program for religious Humanism that many would still accept:

> The time has come for widespread recognition of the radical changes in religious beliefs throughout the modern world. . . . Religions the world over are under the necessity of coming to terms with the new conditions created by a vastly increased knowledge and experience. In every field of human activity, the vital movement is now in the direction of a candid and explicit humanism. In order that religious humanism may be better understood we, the undersigned, desire to make certain affirmations which we believe the facts of our contemporary life demonstrate.
>
> There is great danger of a final, and we believe fatal, identification of the word *religion* with doctrines and methods which have lost their significance and which are powerless to solve the problem of living in the twentieth century. Religions have always been means for realizing the highest values of life. . . . But through all changes religion itself remains constant in its quest for abiding values, an inseparable feature of human life.

After noting the "vast debt" owed to traditional religion, the preamble concludes with a call to establish religion on a new foundation consistent with contemporary knowledge and ethical values: "To establish such a religion is a major necessity of the present."

The fifteen "theses" that constitute the body of the Manifesto are comparatively brief. But for our overview of the document's proposed reconstruction of religion and ethics, the first five theses (on a naturalistic conception of life and the universe) plus the eighth thesis (on the rationale of values), are most relevant:

First: Religious humanists regard the universe as self-existing and not created.

Second: Humanism believes that man is a part of nature and that he emerged as the result of a continuous process.

Third: Holding to an organic view of life, humanists find that the traditional dualism of mind and body must be rejected.

Fourth: Humanism recognizes that man's religious culture and civilization, as clearly depicted by anthropology and history, are the product of a gradual development due to his interaction with his natural environment and with his social heritage. The individual born into a particular culture is largely molded to that culture.

Fifth: Humanism asserts that the nature of the universe depicted by modern science makes unacceptable any supernatural guarantees of human values. Obviously, humanism does not deny the possibility of realities as yet undiscovered, but it does insist that the way to determine the existence and value of any and all realities is by means of intelligent inquiry and by the assessment of their relation to human needs. Religion must formulate its hopes and plans in the light of the scientific spirit and method.

* * *

Eighth: Religious humanism considers the complete realization of the human personality to be the end [purpose or aim] of man's life and seeks its development and fulfillment in the here and now. This is the explanation of the humanist's social passion.

"So stand the theses of religious humanism," declares the Manifesto's conclusion. The document is from first to last the expression of a philosophy that is conceived in explicitly religious terms. Humanist secularism (in the sense of excluding the religious aspect of the Humanist philosophy) is a later divergence within the organized Humanist movement in America.

A comprehensive statement of Humanism from a secularist perspective by a philosopher of note appeared in 1949 with the publication of Corliss Lamont's *Humanism as a Philosophy*. In the frequently reprinted revised editions, published under the title, *The Philosophy of Humanism*, Lamont moderated his position so as to embrace religious as well as secularist expressions of Humanism, although his personal preference remained nonreligious. Lamont's earlier book, *The Illusion of Immortality*, published in 1935, deserves mention as a critique of the concept of individual survival after death and of "evidences" advanced in support of that doctrine.

In recent decades secularists have come to occupy a prominent and respected position on the American Humanist scene, but the impression cultivated by fundamentalist polemicists that the Humanist movement as a whole is nonreligious or even hostile to religion cannot be sustained. The assertion is false, both in terms of history and current membership. It must be remembered that from its inception, and for at least the first generation of its existence, the American Humanist Association served primarily as a publication society and functioned as a support group for Humanists active in liberal churches (primarily Unitarian or Universalist) and Ethical societies. Even today, the majority of people who identify with the Humanist movement in any organizational sense are probably members of such congregations (or of the recently formed Society for Humanistic Judaism, founded by Rabbi Sherwin T. Wine). This fact remains true of many current members of the American Humanist Association and its local and regional chapters. Moreover, Humanism is the common philosophy of a wide range of organizations, as well as of millions of freethinking people unaffiliated with any organized group.

Within the merged Unitarian Universalist denomination, naturalistic Humanism today is ably championed by such eminent ministers as Khoren Arisian in Minneapolis and Paul H. Beattie in Pittsburgh. Beattie has also long served as president of the Fellowship of Religious Humanists, a "bridge" organization that includes many Unitarian Universalist clergy and Ethical Humanist leaders in its membership.

Eminent Humanist thinkers like Julian Huxley, John Dewey, Walter Lippmann, Erich Fromm, and Abraham Maslow have found in the philosophy of Humanistic Naturalism the foundation for a rich religious experience, the potential for a life-enhancing faith grounded in the total human response to the environing universe. We turn now to take a closer look at the Humanist's moral and spiritual quest.

CHAPTER FIVE

Spiritual Values of Ethical Humanism

"If Ethical Culture were not a religion, I would not be interested in it." So remarked David S. Muzzey, a colleague of Felix Adler and late senior leader of the New York Society for Ethical Culture. (Older readers may recall Muzzey as the familiar American historian whose history texts were studied by at least two generations of high school students throughout the nation.)

Professor Muzzey's repeated insistence that to be equal to its task Ethical Culture had to be understood as a religion was still vividly recalled by his recent colleagues when I first became a leader in the movement. Professor Horace Friess and Jerome Nathanson, who had served with Muzzey on the Board of Leaders of the New York society, frequently referred to his earnest religious commitment, a conviction that Friess fully shared but that Nathanson accepted only with reservations.

Had not Adler insisted that the Ethical movement is religious for those who accept it as religious, but purely ethical for those so inclined? Yet Adler always followed up this statement of principle by adding that he counted himself among those who regarded Ethical Culture as their religion. For Muzzey, as for Adler before him, ethical experience took on the quality of religion without necessarily involving any theological assumptions. Late in his life Muzzey underscored this point by entitling one of his books *Ethics as a Religion.*

Adler's insistence that the movement should remain open to the religious and the nonreligious alike is well taken. But the openness and fair-mindedness that Adler called for applies to both sides of the argument. Serious dialogue requires that the genuineness of the nontheistic Humanist's religious convictions be recognized and respected as other sincere professions of religious feeling are treated. Light-minded ridicule of nontheistic religion as "semantic non-sense," somehow comparable to "making a religion of golf or business"—do not do credit to serious discussion.

The nontheistic Humanist who conceives religion as consecration to life values having its ultimate significance expressed in Albert Schweitzer's striking phrase "reverence for life," is not engaged in straining the meaning of language. It is the element of consecration—of treating an exalted principle as sacred—that characterizes religion in all cultures and ages.

Nontheistic religions exist and have a long and honorable history. No survey of the major types of religious philosophy from ancient to modern times can be comprehensive without the inclusion of a number of such nontheistic faiths of both East and West. Some culture-bound authorities, addicted exclusively to the Judeo-Christian type of theistic religion, will insist on prefacing an account of Hinayana Buddhism (the south Asian variety that remains most faithful to early Buddhist thought), or of Zen or comparable nontheistic systems of faith, with the contention that they are not "strictly" religious because they are not based on belief in a deity. But such scholars nevertheless find it necessary to include these nontheistic beliefs among the great faiths of humanity.

"But why bother with such a troublesome and ambiguous

word as religion?" demands the secularist. Why not be satisfied with calling Ethical Humanism a philosophy? The shortest answer is the most direct: We call Ethical Humanism a religion because it feels like a religion, wears like a religion, and serves as a religion. It occupies in our lives a place identical to that which other faith-commitments occupy in the lives of our neighbors. No other term describes in its fullness the spiritual resonance that John Dewey identified as "the religious quality of experience."

Moreover, we have observed that when groups rule out the concept of "the religious" and "religion" as applying to themselves, they tend to neglect, and even scorn, those very qualities of experience we most prize as characterizing the spiritual life: the qualities of reverence, adoration, and consecrated devotion to life's sacred character. Those who experience the world religiously will need no further description of what these qualities of experience are like or of their incomparable value in rendering ultimate meaning to human existence. Despite the commonplace opinion to the contrary, the argument is not merely one of "semantics." The issue is one of basic attitude and orientation. When we repress the familiar language that best communicates our spiritual aspirations and feelings, we are as handicapped as a lover of the arts would be if all the terms peculiar to aesthetic experience were stricken from the vocabulary of beauty and form. We might still have our inner experience, but it could not be informed or reinforced by the like experience of others.

In fact, the argument as to whether Humanism is a philosophy or a religion misses the essential point. Surely we can accede to the proposition that Humanism is a philosophy. But it is a philosophy that contains, at least in embryo, the soul of a living faith. A comprehensive worldview, as the Humanist philosophy surely is, will have something fresh and original to contribute to our understanding of the nature of religious experience. As a comprehensive reconception of the nature and structure of knowledge, including moral and spiritual knowledge, Humanist naturalism contains the potential for the radical reconstruction of religious thought and feeling. Religious Humanists are intellectually and spiritually committed to that reconstruction.

Each major discipline or field of knowledge has its own specialized application of philosophy. The philosophy of religion is such a discipline. As soon as we begin *to think* about religion, we are unavoidably propelled into questions that constitute the philosophy of religion. So, even if we took the position (which we do not) that Humanism excludes the possibility of being religious on its own terms, we would still find ourselves developing a philosophy of religion by which to explain (if only to refute) the phenomenon of religion in human life and history. But to dismiss religious feeling as the product of pure illusion and error strains credulity. Feuerbach appreciated this fact when he set about the task of analyzing religious behavior and belief in terms of the fundamental attributes and dynamics of human consciousness. In short, religion rests on human foundations, not on any particular metaphysical or theological structure. This recognition is what religious Humanism is all about.

Whether one particularly approves or not, religion exists as a fact of universal human history. A God or gods may not exist outside the realm of human imagination. The world of supernatural powers may be a chimera. But the category of intangible values, feelings, forebodings, aspirations, commitments, and relationships that human beings have experienced immemorially as religious, worshipful, sacred, or "holy" is part of the psychosocial makeup of our species. That quality of experience pervades and infuses our most cherished associations and interactions.

One may dismiss all of the beliefs and dogmas that are popularly associated with particular religions as mere superstitions. Many thought they had succeeded in banishing religious sentiments—only to discover that they still retained feelings of awe, reverence, and "a sense of the sacred," now focused on the sanctity of life itself. This quality of experience, its nature and value in human living, constitutes the perennial and universal subject matter of the philosophy of religion, transcending any particular mythology, theology, or religious type.

A contemporary Ethical Humanist leader, Arthur Dobrin, has observed:

> As we interact with our surroundings, we come to know the sacred. Life becomes precious as we treat it with great care. The earth becomes sacred as we relate to it as something to be replenished by our efforts. The attitude of respect creates the religious dimension.

Dobrin argues that the sense of "the holy"—which the German theologian Rudolph Otto contended is the common denominator of religious experience—is to be found within the world of everyday relationships made transcendent by human dedication. "Holiness is not found elsewhere," Dobrin declares, "but *right here* [emphasis added]. It is available as we seek it in the spirit of love and respect."

Ethical Humanism, in Dobrin's view, constitutes a distinctive middle way between the extremes of other-worldly mysticism and nonreligious secularism. "For secularists," he writes, "nothing is sacred; for mystics, everything. Ethical Humanists, by contrast, hold that holiness is created by the manner in which a person meets the world." His view closely parallels that of Julian Huxley in identifying religion with experience of the sacred, which in Huxley's view can attach to any number of natural objects, values, and relationships.

While conceding that worship of the supernatural is one

of the most familiar forms of religion, Huxley argued that "belief in supernatural beings is not an essential or integral part of the religious way of life nor, conversely, are the objects of religious feeling necessarily supernatural beings." He contended:

> I believe, then, that religion arose as a feeling of the sacred. The capacity for experiencing this feeling in relation to various objects and events seems to be a fundamental capacity of man, something given in and by the construction of the normal human mind, just as definitely as is the capacity for experiencing anger or admiration, sympathy or terror.

Julian Huxley's Religion of Evolutionary Humanism

Labeling his reconception of religion "Evolutionary Humanism," Huxley stressed a developmental process of historical growth. "Regarded as progress," he wrote in the 1957 revised edition of *Religion Without Revelation* (from which the quotations above are also taken), "the history of religion is the purging of the religious emotion itself from baser elements such as fear, and the substitution of ever larger, nobler, and more rational objects and situations."

In its early conception of reality, according to Huxley's thought, religion "concerns itself mainly with putting man right with objects or beings regarded as imbued with sacred power," but as thought advances through history, "in its later stages its most urgent desire is to gain the quality of holiness for the man himself, and to arrive . . . at an assurance of personal salvation."

For Huxley, the religious naturalist, as for the psychoanalyst, Erich Fromm, who also wrote sympathetically of religion from a nontheistic Humanist perspective, salvation is to be found here on earth in the attainment of personal wholeness and fulfillment. Thus, for both Huxley and Fromm, the goal of inner healing and the realization of lasting spiritual composure are to be discovered within the ethical and humanistic, to be attained in relationship to one's self and others and in the progression of the generations through history.

As a working Ethical leader who has the spiritual well-being of his Society membership as a primary professional concern, Dobrin has recorded the importance of social bonds and historical continuities in nurturing the inner self:

> Everywhere people seek a sense of connection, a feeling of continuity between the past and the present. While living in the past can prevent living in the present, it is also true that without these connections we become like words without a story. . . . It is in the structure of our connectedness that we are linked to the past, to others and to ourselves, as well as to the passage of time and to eternity.

"Thus," wrote Huxley, in much the same vein, "a developed religion should definitely be a relation of the personality to the whole of the universe." Such a relationship would be "one into which reverence enters and one in which the ultimate satisfactions of discovering and knowing truth, experiencing and expressing beauty, and ensuing the good . . . all have the freest possible play."

For Julian Huxley, as for perhaps all spiritual pathfinders and pioneers, attention to the call of religious sensibility was more than a matter of scoring points in an intellectual game. Critics might review the work of such a spirit from an analytical and purely cognitive perspective, and Huxley himself possessed a sharply honed scientific mind that was acutely attuned to the intellectual and critical aspects of his religious quest. This was sufficient to separate him from traditional conceptions of theology and to turn his thought in the direction of a philosophy of religious naturalism that he called Humanism.

But the enterprise itself had a more immediate and earnest motivation. Religious feeling was central to his sensitivity and joie de vivre. When a precariously balanced nervous constitution deprived him of the emotional energy to respond appreciatively to the world around him, and extinguished his inner consciousness of being alive in such a universe, Huxley fell into incapacitating depression.

In his autobiography, *Memories*, which he completed in his eightieth year, Huxley described a lifelong battle with periods of emotional breakdown that interrupted his scientific work and personal life. Soon after his marriage he fell into one of these spells of depression that, he recorded, frightened and dismayed his Swiss bride, Juliette, who had no previous knowledge of such a malady as a nervous breakdown. But the even-tempered and resourceful young wife, whom he had first met when she served as a governess in a British household, learned soon enough what severe depression can do to a person—and helped her brilliant but emotionally fragile husband through several similar bouts of emotional illness during the fifty-six years of their lives together.

Julian attributed his nervous temperament to his mother's family, the Arnolds, and especially to the genes he had inherited from his grandfather, Thomas Arnold, eccentric brother of the celebrated poet and literary critic, Matthew Arnold, and second son of the educator, Thomas Arnold, headmaster of Rugby. Julian's brother Trevenen—midway in age between Julian and their youngest brother, Aldous— had taken his life after an unhappy love affair. Julian recollected that at the time he could not grasp why Trev had forsaken a future so filled with promise. Later he understood, and reproached himself for not lending greater psychological support to his brother during the breakdown and hospitalization that ended in his suicide.

Perhaps Julian would have taken the same approach to Humanism as a religion without these desperate experiences. Certainly his temperament and interests, as well as the religious speculations of his Huxley grandfather, pointed him in the direction of a religious faith consistent with his scientific interests and beliefs. Aldous also came to have a lifelong preoccupation with unconventional religious thought, especially with mysticism as a universal aspect of religion that he found to be remarkably constant in conception and practice across all cultural boundaries. Nevertheless, Julian's psychological crises and the observations and reflections that these episodes inspired give to his religious writings authority and power. His extended and trying convalescences turned his attention toward books that eventually spurred the writing of *Religion Without Revelation*.

> My nervous breakdown in 1912, [he wrote] . . . had inflicted on me "the dark night of the soul," in which all sense of fruitful communion, in human love, or with natural and man-made beauty, and even in fruitful moral or intelligent co-operation, went overboard. The essentially religious feeling of oneness with nature, with art and with my fellow-beings, was lost. Even the consolation of work was denied to me.

While teaching at Rice Institute (now Rice University) in Texas, Huxley gradually recovered from one such crisis and, as he wrote, "renewed my enjoyment of work and natural beauty, and of human company." Another illness at a hospital in Colorado Springs gave him time and inclination to read the essays of John Morley where he encountered the great English liberal's philosophical reflections on science and religion. Morley had suggested that "the next great task of science will be to create a religion for humanity." Shades of Auguste Comte! Only Morley was obviously looking for something more in keeping with the spirit of liberal idealism and scientific free thought than Comte's rigidly conceived "Religion of Humanity" would allow. (Huxley learned afterward that a suggestion similar to Morley's had also been made by the French philologist and religious historian, Ernest Renan, whose human conception of Jesus, popularized in his best-selling *Life of Jesus,* had considerably agitated Christian orthodoxy.)

Influences closer to home also affected Julian. We have already mentioned the evolutionary ethics of his grandfather, T. H. Huxley, who had coined the word "agnostic" to describe an attitude of suspended judgment toward the question of God's existence. Having at least equal bearing on Julian's turn toward religious Humanism was the idealism of his Aunt Mary, who had always been close to the Huxley brothers and became a virtual second mother to the younger brothers, Trev and Aldous, following the death of her sister.

Julian's Aunt Mary, who as a noted novelist wrote under her married name, Mrs. Humphrey Ward, shared the family's skepticism of Christian supernaturalism. But she suggested the possibility of a creedless religion of good deeds. In her novel, *Robert Elsmere,* an Anglican cleric renounces his faith to become a benevolent worker among the poor, inspired by human love and compassion. Huxley responded to the impact of his aunt's novel on his developing religious consciousness when, following the lead of Lord Morley, he outlined his proposal for a religion of Evolutionary Humanism. Of that development he wrote:

> Earlier my aunt Mary Ward's book, *Robert Elsmere,* had made a deep impression on me, and helped to convert me to what I must call a religious humanism, but without belief in any personal God.
> In 1927, this book, in combination with Morley's words, prompted me to undertake a book on religion in general.

The outcome of this resolution was a work that immediately brought wide attention to the claims of Humanism as a religion—as Huxley suggested, *the* coming great world religion. The book remains a classic of Humanist thought and faith. *Religion Without Revelation* remained in print with periodic revision for the nearly fifty years of life that remained to Huxley. To this principal work he added other volumes setting forth the case for Evolutionary Humanism as a religion without God. *Man Stands Alone* and *The Humanist Frame* are notable examples of the development of his thought.

Huxley's profound spiritual sensibility came through especially during the latter decades of his life. Without abandoning his naturalistic premises, he deepened his conception of spirituality as an innate quality of human consciousness. In an address delivered in 1956 to the Bristol Meeting of the Ethical Union in Britain, a lecture later incorporated as a new chapter in the subsequent edition of *Religion Without Revelation,* Huxley considered the idea of God from a cultural and scientific perspective.

"The god hypothesis," he argued, is no longer of any pragmatic value for the interpretation or comprehension of nature, and indeed often stands in the way of a better and truer interpretation."

We hear echoes of T. H. Huxley's century-old argument that biological evolution, holding center stage in past ages, now gives way to a new stage of evolution—cultural evolution, in which ideas and customs that equip human society for survival become crucial. The elder Huxley saw the evolution of ethics as such an instrument.

Julian applied a parallel thought to religion, which he contended serves as an "organ" of adjustment to human destiny "considered in the light of our sense of its essential sacredness and inevitable mystery." By tying religion to what he saw as antiquated beliefs—particularly beliefs about gods or God—we jeopardize the future of the religious function as it relates to its essentially human task.

"The time is ripe," he said to the Ethical Union delegates gathered in Bristol, "for the dethronement of gods from their dominant position in our interpretation of destiny, in favor of a naturalistic type of belief-system." It would soon become "impossible for an intelligent, educated man or woman to believe in a god." Then, recognizing that this anticipation was far from inevitable, he added: "However, this will not happen unless the emerging naturalistic type of belief is fully adequate to its task."

Certain totalitarian belief systems that functioned as surrogate religions provided examples as types not to be followed: "The two most obvious are Nazism in Germany and Marxist Communism in Russia." Nazism was "inherently self-destructive" and "grotesquely incorrect" as an interpretation of destiny, "analogous to some of the primitive products of the theistic type, such as deified beasts, bloodthirsty tribal deities, or revengeful divine beasts." Communism was "more competent," but limited by its denial of "the reality of spiritual values." As a result, the Soviet authorities "have had to accept the consequences of their ideological error, and grudgingly throw the churches open to the multitudes seeking the spiritual values which had been excluded from their system."

The thirty years that have elapsed since Huxley voiced these observations have not seen the weakening of theistic belief systems. The adequacy of naturalistic alternatives has not been demonstrated except within numerically small circles of religious liberals who take seriously the spiritual component of Humanism that Huxley believed essential. Fundamentalism and religious reaction against the sterility of a "value-free" positivism in science and technology have arisen around the world. Purely materialistic and secularist belief systems, even when encouraged by the state, as in the Soviet Union, have proved to have little hold on the human spirit, thriving only as short-lived protests against corrupted and oppressive religious orthodoxies. A stronger case for religious freedom and tolerance can hardly be made.

Huxley was always at pains to distinguish his Evolutionary Humanism from the scientifically minded secularism popular among self-styled rationalists. "I had long been a member of the Rationalist Press Association," he wrote, but found their attitude too rational and materialistic, too much concerned with attacking churches and picking holes in religious dogmas, while discounting the value of any religious or mystical experience." His reference was to 1927, the year he wrote *Religion Without Revelation*.

Some thirty years later the Rationalist Press Association joined with the Ethical Union in Britain (which had departed from the religious emphasis of the American movement) to become the British Humanist Association. Clearly, Huxley's Humanism was more in accord with the trans-Atlantic religious Humanism of the United States and Canada than with the course of events in his own country. When in 1952 the American Ethical Union and the American Humanist Association collaborated with their counterparts in Europe to found the International and Ethical Union, Huxley was the obvious choice to serve as the honorary chair of the world organization.

Naturalistic Humanism's Contribution to Nontheistic Religion

As we have seen, Julian Huxley was only one of many major scientific figures of the past half-century to advocate naturalistic Humanism as an alternative to orthodox theism or other supernaturalist belief systems. He was already an eminent biologist when at the age of forty he wrote *Religion Without Revelation*. Yet his major theoretical work, updating and broadening the conception of evolution, which would win him a permanent place in the history of science, lay fifteen or more years in the future. The Synthetic Theory, as it has come to be known, a synthesis of Darwinian natural selection with the principles of genetics discovered since Darwin's time, remolded evolutionary theory and put the understanding of evolution on a firmer, more credible conceptual foundation. Still, Huxley insisted that he and his science remained firmly Darwinian. As one of the principal architects of "the modern synthesis," Huxley proved to be a worthy descendent of his grandfather, a forceful exponent of the legacy of Charles Darwin.

His study of religion as a cultural "organ" for the development and transmission of values associated with human destiny and feelings of the sacred, was an integral aspect of his inquiry into the behavior of social species, as well as an example of his intellectual powers in organizing data into fruitful hypotheses. Even so, significant as his work was on both sides of the Atlantic in promoting a Humanist outlook in scientific and popular circles, the influence of his Evolutionary Humanism in America was secondary to that of the pragmatic philosophy of John Dewey and others associated with the development of humanistic naturalism. We shall turn to their work later, especially with respect to the theory of moral creativity and consider how their thinking related to the earlier ethical idealism of Felix Adler and his associates in the early Ethical movement.

One further observation, however, is pertinent in our review of the development of religious Humanism. Huxley's scientifically inspired religious quest, despite his scrupulous restraint as a self-critical observer, often soars into a full-blown nature mysticism, making his work singularly prophetic for an age newly sensititized to our human niche in the ecology of a living earth. Naturalism of the type he represented, permeated as it is with reverence for natural creativity and beauty, imbued with an overpowering consciousness of human connectedness within the evolving web of life, engenders a celebrative religion of cosmic piety—

no weaker term will do—that gives wings to the human spirit as no abstract moral philosophy can.

Thus Huxley's vision brought strength to religious Humanism at the very point where existing systems of ethical idealism tended to be weakest. This applies—with some qualification—to Felix Adler's conception of ethical faith as well as to similar schools of idealism. Although Adler personally had a keen appreciation of nature, spending long summer retreats in his study high in the Adirondacks, all too little of his love of nature or his awareness of our place in the great community of life comes through in his writings. The absence of such a note was not a mere personal lapse. The fault lay rather in the limitations of his philosophy. At least that had been Goethe's criticism of Kant's abstract intellectualism a century before Adler's time, and Adler stood consciously in Kant's philosophical line of succession.

What Goethe had deplored in Kant's system of idealism was its lofty rationalism, its unease with the concrete, the particular, and the sensuous; its setting beyond arm's reach the consolations and transforming epiphanies of the flesh; its exaggerated distrust of passion, anguish, joy, and the life-giving ecstasy of the rare, precious moments of spiritual fullness and self-realization. In his famous conversations with Schiller, Goethe persuaded the younger thinker that his work would achieve greater directness and power if he removed his Kantian spectacles and saw nature afresh.

Beyond his "dark night of the soul," and fortified by childhood memories of the English countryside explored with his beloved "Gran'pater," Julian Huxley developed a religious sensibility for nature that became the guiding star of his scientific work as well as the light of his inner spirit. A reverence for the universe having the aura of the mystical drove his passion to understand the natural world—to know it conceptually as a scientist and to hold it imaginatively as a lover and worshipper. He thus re-created the same essentially religious feeling for truth that on quite different theological foundations had motivated Kepler, Newton, and other classic heroes of modern science. In Huxley's own age, Einstein, Eddington, Jeans, Bronowski, and others of similar sensibility—theists and nontheists alike—were to acknowledge "the religious quality of experience" that illumined their introspections.

It was this dynamic of natural reverence that a developing ethical religion needed most to correct its overreliance on the abstractions of rationalistic idealism. Huxley was only the most indefatigible of many twentieth-century men and women of science to articulate this quality of experience, which John Dewey was to identify as "the religious" and the theologian Paul Tillich acknowledged to be an authentic religious type described as "natural piety." Einstein—the greatest of them all—was to testify to the transcendent values of the scientific pursuit itself, its intellectual rigor, ethical integrity, artistic creativity, and finally its moments of distinctively religious luminosity.

The Ethical Humanist religious sensibility that has emerged from this history is the product of the two great streams of ethical idealism, exemplified in Kant's and Adler's exalted moral philosophies, and of religious naturalism, manifest in the spiritual reflections of the Huxleys, Dewey, and Einstein, and in the psychological studies of Fromm, Rogers, and Maslow, among others.

Where does this leave our conception of the spiritual life, our reformulation of the Ethical Humanist religious sensibility? Reduced to its core, with its extraneous cultural husks stripped away, the religious experience is essentially the culmination and summit of our perception of connectedness and continuity. It is the experience of being caught up in life's most sustaining and self-transcending relationships—which at their climactic moments cease to be perceived as mere external relations and assume the aspect of an inner unity, an immersion of the ego into a more comprehensive, enveloping whole.

In the literature of religious psychology, peak experiences are called "spiritual," or even "mystical" when the unifying or "beatific" vision attains the fullness of the cosmic and the timeless—conceptions that overleap the ordinary and habitual boundaries of the self. If one believes in a transcendent God and thereby interprets these experiences in theistic terms, the mystical experience is interpreted as the union of the self with God. But if one thinks in other than traditional theistic terms, the unifying vision may encompass whatever is conceived to be experientially ultimate, as supreme in value and meaning. (The Humanist psychologist, Abraham Maslow, popularized the concept of the "peak experience" and helped especially to make the realm of religious feeling comprehensible in naturalistic terms.) The experience is one of "beatitude" and fulfillment, in which the world of ordinary relationships is transvalued and made complete. For the Humanist, life itself is pregnant with such experiences of transcendence.

Such moments are rare and fleeting. Their value lies in their power to strengthen, focus, and enlarge our conception of existence and reality and so to provide a deeper, more stable and more secure footing in confronting the inevitable trials and traumas of living. For minds alive to this sensibility religious experience is essentially the realization of transcendence, not transcendence in the absolute sense of escape to another and better world, but in the relative sense of a transvaluation of the world we have, of finding a fulcrum that provides stability and leverage to the thrust of one's life. Far from being escapist, as many fear, these are qualities that deepen perspective and strengthen the will.

Writing as a scientist and religious freethinker, Jacob

Bronowski explored the significance of the unitary vision of the artist and mystic (using William Blake as his primary example) and found a comparable quality in the most inspired moments of creativity in science. In Bronowski's view, the artist, religious prophet, and scientist in their creative imagination are not doing radically different things; they are doing essentially the same thing. The bolder and more comprehensive their insight, Brownowski contended, the more completely the scientist and artist resemble each other in the quality of their creativity.

The rise of a renewed sense of transcendence, appearing just when many contemporary intellectuals thought all spiritual vitality was in final retreat, has many causes, ranging from the revolution in physics and logic that has dethroned mechanistic materialism and determinism, to the global crisis in social structures and morality. Certain of the impulses that have elevated the hunger for the transcendent in human life are regressive. But others deserve to be recognized as genuinely affirmative and humanistic.

Julian Huxley, who warned us thirty-five years ago of the growing "recrudescence" of irrational and authoritarian ways of thinking, understood both the promise and the threat of an age of science to intellectual and spiritual freedom. If a rational and reasonable faith is not available to human beings—if what is offered is not spiritually adequate—civilization will be turned toward a new dark age of superstition and mind control. An adequate Ethical Humanism is one that nurtures equally the intellectual and spiritual vigor of human beings. Such a faith must acknowledge the necessary poles of the life of the mind— the intellectual and the spiritual—not as opposing forces, but as dynamically interdependent.

A retired senior leader of the New York Society, Dr. Sheldon Ackley, has described Ethical religion as "a spiritual alternative for Humanists." Another Ethical leader of national influence, Jean Somerville Kotkin, has summed up the task of humanistic religion with the observation that "beyond material help and beyond even intellectual help, there is a third service needed by humankind. That is the revelation of the spiritual life and potentialities of humanity. That is our faith."

CHAPTER SIX

The Secret of Moral Creativity

Horace Friess was fond of saying that Ethical Culture consisted of three interrelated parts: religious, educational, and social. Professor Friess was in a position to know. He was a longtime student of the Ethical movement, a distinguished professor of philosophy at Columbia, a member of the Board of Leaders of the New York Society for Ethical Culture, and the biographer of his father-in-law, Felix Adler.

Yet it would be difficult for anyone even casually familiar with Ethical Culture to avoid his conclusion, which is obvious when we examine the life of the movement. From the beginning Ethical Culture was committed to social justice and practical reform. Similarly, when the Society was only two years old, it initiated in 1878 the educational program that grew into the widely studied and admired Ethical Culture Schools of New York.

Adler's influence in education, political reform, social work among the poor, and for international peace with racial and economic justice extended far beyond the religious movement known as Ethical Culture. If we have devoted the first half of this study to the philosophical and religious underpinnings of Ethical Humanism, we have done so because the moral and spiritual vision of Ethical Religion is the mainspring of its effective practical action in education and social involvement. But there was never any question in Adler's mind: the proof of the faith is in its living. A spirituality that does not struggle to improve the world is not spiritual at all. It is merely self-deceiving sanctimony and bathos. For good reason Ethical Humanism has been called "religion in work clothes."

Nevertheless, it must always be borne in mind that in asserting that Ethical Humanism is a religious, educational, and social movement we are not saying that it is made up of three separate interests somehow compressed into one. On the contrary, it is a single integral process of creative spiritual growth having religious, educational, and social consequences. To minimize or inhibit any one of these cohering and coordinate qualities would be to truncate and diminish the other two.

As an educational movement, Ethical Humanism touches the vital core of the creative interaction that shapes our humanity. We understand ethics not as mere rule making but as a dynamic principle that enables moral and spiritual development to occur. Understanding this process discloses the secret for achieving a spiritually rich and free community of whole and mature persons. This does not mean, of course, that members of Ethical Societies always achieve this goal. The process of ethical growth must be faithfully lived to be effective. As Ethical Humanists we do not necessarily have the inside track over others who may apply the principles of ethical living more effectively. We can, however, begin by taking the promising step of recognizing that creative moral living is the final source of all the qualities that make us human.

All religions attempt to relate human consciousness to those primary forces that are perceived to be the sources and sustainers of our being. The most primitive gods were scarcely veiled personifications of such inner and outer powers in the world. The question of sources is essential to illuminate the dynamic, generative core of moral and spiritual development. Keeping this thought in mind, we are enabled to see the logic of the contention, argued earlier, that the religious quality of life is not an additive or an ornament superimposed upon ethical experience, but is an aspect of the very structure and essence of the morally creative process that shapes what we are and contains the potential for what we can become.

Again we emphasize that there is nothing inherent in the idea of a creative source or power that compels us to leap to a supernaturalistic or theistic explanation. That "logical necessity" is pure habit, a holdover of cultural conditioning, and nothing more. We can just as logically assume (and without multiplying regressive "unknowns") that the universe or cosmic system is a self-contained, self-operating order that has existed eternally in some form or aspect of its being. The argument about the two competing ideas—divine creation *versus* a self-existing cosmos—has been debated endlessly without resolution. Both propositions are beyond even theoretical demonstration. Many logicians contend that talk about such unverifiable questions is inherently nonsensical and devoid of any possible meaning.

Religious naturalists treat the "natural" universe as an independent, self-contained system because our knowledge of the world, as Kant brilliantly demonstrated two centuries ago, is totally confined to events within the world itself. We can describe parts of the world in relational terms— how they affect each other—but we have no way of defining or grasping the "being" of the whole. In recognizing this limit to all our knowledge, contemporary naturalism and the philosophy of science accept Kant's reasoning. In fact, contemporary naturalists argue that they apply Kant's principle more consistently and rigorously than he could do, since he was misled by the now discredited assumption, believed in his day to be firmly established, that mathematical logic discloses the fixed physical structure of the universe and that space and time are absolute. Recognition since Kant's day of alternative logical systems, giving rise to non-Euclidean geometry, and Einstein's theory of relativity have made both absolutes untenable.

A logically consistent naturalism simply accepts the universe as given, recognizing that what we know or can know about external reality must always be confined within the limits of finite events and relationships contained within nature itself. There is no conceivable way—not even in principle—for us to step "outside" that naturalistic frame to look beyond the phenomenal world. All knowledge of the external world is therefore relative.

This brings us back to an assumption that recurs throughout this book. For the religious naturalist or Humanist, the sources of our being must be located within the familiar realm of time and space, in nature, in evolutionary and cultural history, and in the context of the sustaining relationships of human beings living in community with one another and the world. It is in this sense of being "in the world" that we earlier described Humanism and related naturalistic philosophies as "secular"—which literally means "in the world." At the same time, we rejected the view that Humanism is necessarily "secularist," in the now common usage of opposing or excluding religion from its vision of life.

The philosophical and religious naturalist refuses to divert human idealism and effort to the vain and untestable attempt to account for the existence of reality as a whole by postulating some external "divine" or "supernatural" power that, as popular religious supernaturalism contends, must be propitiated and worshipped. The naturalist sees no ground for supposing such a being to exist, or for investing human resources in pursuit of a will-of-the-wisp so footless in logic or meaning.

We turn instead to find the knowable sources of our being within the interactive creative process that is life. But even this conception is too broad if we wish to discover the character of the moral factor in human creation. Here we must be much more selective in identifying the factors in nature and nurture that support the emergence of moral and spiritual values and sustain them in human relationships. If this were not so, we could relax in the assurance of a benevolent pantheism, finding the divine goodness equally distributed in all things. But if the whole of things actualizes God, the whole of things just as certainly expresses Satan. Such misty fantasies do not carry us far in understanding the moral creativity we seek in order to maximize the good life, or to affirm the moral worth of persons.

Religious naturalism does not deify the universe. Nature as a whole is blind and prodigiously wasteful of life. With Albert Schweitzer we are horrified by much that is manifest in nature. To pretend that the "real" is good, while evil is "illusory" or is merely deprived of the good—an explanation as old as ancient Greek philosophy—simply evades the problem. Even those who profess to see final moral perfection in the cosmos are sure to take their flu shots and wear their rubbers in inclement weather. Nature is not uniformly "friendly," and to the degree that it is friendly at all, it is so because all viable life forms have evolved means of coping with the hostile and destructive forces that confront them in the struggle for survival. We see evidence of this fact throughout the biological world and do not look to the universe any more than we look to a transcendent God to safeguard our lives or guarantee our values. Thus our religious naturalism does not make us nature worshippers. On the contrary, it innoculates us from the worship of "forces" and "powers" of whatever guise.

What then is left that is worthy of human veneration and reverence? What remains is the moral and spiritual potential to achieve the good within our relationships, within our actions and attitudes toward each other, and within ourselves. To understand this in the most radical, fundamental terms is to discover the necessity for the ethical life to be morally and spiritually self-contained and self-generative. We can rely on no props external to the moral process itself. Indeed, no such props are possible except at the price of illusion and self-deception.

Viewed in this light, Schweitzer's inspired phrase, "reverence for life," acquires a deeper meaning. Not only do we reverence life by feeling compassion and empathy for its concrete forms; but, more fundamentally, through reverence for life we see life as a precarious but infinitely precious creative process pregnant with the meanings that give to human existence the only enduring values that we can know.

Ethical Humanism, grounded in a this-worldly conception of the forces and conditions that sustain moral development, finds no merit in postulating a supermundane Heaven as the repository of our ultimate life values. The theory of ethical creativity presented here reflects elements that were common to the thinking of Felix Adler, John Dewey, the religious naturalist Henry Nelson Wieman (who somewhat confusingly called his concept "naturalistic theism"), and more recently, the psychologists Erich Fromm, Abraham Maslow, Carl Rogers, and others. However much these thinkers may have differed among themselves on certain logical and metaphysical issues that were important to their technical philosophies, they spoke with a single voice in affirming the interpersonal process as the generative source of moral development—the creator of the whole spectrum of qualities that make us human and give us the ability to assimilate and express all the "higher" attributes of the spiritual, aesthetic, and intellectual life.

Interaction, transaction, and interchange are the key terms that sprinkle the pages of their writings on how values are generated in human life. Community precedes individuality. There is no possibility for individuality to develop—for personal maturation to occur to any significant extent—without supportive social relations. Community may be as intimate as that between two people, beginning with the first interaction between mother and child. In order to work, the relationship must be genuinely interactive. It cannot be a one-way street with the parent only giving and the child merely receiving. From the beginning the infant responds in significant ways, so that the life experience of the mother (or other significant adult) is enlarged even as the infant develops through the experience. Experiments done with young animals have shown the irreparable damage caused to any of the higher social animals by depriving the individual in infancy of interaction with a caring "parent."

Felix Adler understood this clearly enough from his study of educational innovations that had been tested by Johann Pestalozzi and others in the experimental schools of Europe. He did not make the original discovery, but to Adler must go much credit for grasping the importance of the principle demonstrated not only for formal education but for religion and the whole of life. The interpersonal theory of value, built firmly on Kant's principle of the absolute worth of the person, provided Adler with the working model he required.

Reformulating Kant's moral maxim (the famous categorical imperative) to give the fullest play to the mutual enhancement of life by unlike individuals in creative interaction, Adler framed his version of the supreme commandment: "Act so as to elicit in others the distinctive excellence characteristic of each of them as fellow members of the ethical whole, and thereby to elicit that excellence more fully in yourself." This formulation, complicated though it may seem as a restatement of the golden rule, is clearer and more guarded in its prescription than the simpler and more familiar version that we have previously cited: "Act so as to elicit the best in others and thereby in thyself."

The simpler version of Adler's dictum lends itself to misunderstanding, suggesting to some people the very opposite of what Adler intended: "Who am I to force my notion of what's best upon someone else?" But read the full formulation again! Adler recognized that the familiar Golden Rule, whether attributed to Jesus, Confucius, or other ancient sages, had the same problem: "I know what is best for you, and I should activate that best." Adler was unsparing in his effort to establish the thought that our highest obligation to others is to encourage "the distinctive excellence" that is the best realizable within each, without prescribing what that distinctive excellence must be. He reworked his moral maxim until he was satisfied that he had gotten it right. That he succeeded is manifested in the recognition since given in education and moral philosophy to individual uniquenesses and the greater attention shown for the rights and freedoms that personal growth requires. While others were eventually much more influential than Adler, especially John Dewey and his associates, Adler's contribution as an educator came early and was prophetic. Dewey was generous in recognizing Adler's achievement.

Misconceptions About Situational and Relative Ethics

Much controversy swirls around the concept of "situationalism" in ethics, and the moral and religious philosophers of Humanism and related schools of thought have been demagogically blamed for corrupting society for allegedly teaching that there are no universally binding ethical standards, or as many express it, "no absolutes." This allegation is confused and false. To say that ethical principles are "relative" is not to deny that they point to something real in human life. Similarly, to contend that ethical judgments must be situational is only to recognize that certain acts must be judged to be right or wrong, good or bad, because they occur in a context giving them particular consequences that might not obtain under quite different circumstances. Therefore, when enemies of Humanism equate the "situation ethics" of Joseph Fletcher and other Humanist philosophers with narcissism, subjectivism, and ultimately with moral nihilism, they simply betray a failure to grasp what situation ethics means. Some Protestant fundamentalists, for example, have spread the notion that Humanist ethics means, "If it feels good, do it." Such a rule, of course, would not even qualify as a guide to rational self-interest, much less serve as a humanistic principle that recognizes the equal rights of others.

Fundamentalist believers might be instructed to learn that St. Paul was among the early practitioners of situation ethics. He advised his Christian followers to abstain from eating meat that had been "sacrificed" to idols (meat that in keeping with pagan custom had been blessed by presentation on the altar of a god). There was nothing inherently wrong with eating such meat, Paul conceded, since Christians did not regard the pagan gods as having any reality. But because the practice might influence a weak member of the faith to relapse into paganism, the apostle advised against it.

Many of the dietary prohibitions of the ancient Hebrews had a similar rationale. The religious authorities forbade certain foods or combinations of foods to discourage primitive rituals that they were determined to stamp out. For example, an orthodox Jew today abstains from eating meat and dairy products at the same meal because the scripture forbids boiling a kid in its mother's milk—an echo of ancient sacrificial ritual. These acts in their original setting led to consequences that were either inhumane (or more often) judged to be disruptive to the religious solidarity of a community. Yet, today they would entail no such consequences, and liberal Jews have modified or abandoned these ancient rules.

Much confusion also arises from the careless and uninformed use of the word "relative" in referring to ethical judgments. To say that ethical values and judgments are relative is to assert that they are related to a particular culture, religious code, or community standard. Anthropologists have described the radically different ways in which various societies have regarded particular behaviors. We all know that for a Mormon a century ago to have more than one wife was regarded as shocking and immoral by non-Mormon American society. Yet the Mormons were correct in pointing out that polygamy was honored in the days of the Hebrew patriarchs as an institution sanctioned by God.

It is a misuse of the concept of the cultural relativity of ethics to apply it to individual conduct in order to argue the point, as some contend, that "right and wrong are only matters of personal opinion." This reduces ethics to a question of personal taste. This may be an increasingly commonplace attitude in contemporary society, but it is hardly an example of moral relativism. It certainly does not qualify as Humanism in any serious sense. Humanists do not subscribe, as we have already noted, to moral nihilism, which makes the desires and immediate self-will of the individual, or a select group, the sole judge of right and wrong behavior. As John Dewey observed, everything that is desired is not desirable. Ethics consists of making that assumption.

In its fourth thesis, the Humanist Manifesto of 1933 acknowledged the fact of cultural relativism in the evolution of religion and ethics:

> Humanism recognizes that man's religious culture and civilization, as clearly depicted by anthropology and history, are the product of a gradual development due to his in-

teraction with his natural environment and with his social heritage. The individual born into a particular culture is largely molded by that culture.

To acknowledge cultural relativity as a fact of social history is not to say that all ethical systems are equally defensible from the standpoint of a normative (prescriptive, or norm-setting) morality. A society that practices cannibalism is understandable in terms of the evolution of human civilization. But from the standpoint of a moral philosophy (such as Ethical Humanism) such a disregard for human life cannot be condoned.

There is no contradiction in the sympathetic understanding of a moral system in terms of its closed historical setting and in stipulating those essential standards and principles that are necessary for human beings to meet their moral obligations as members of a society committed to the propositions of moral equality and human dignity. As Ethical Humanists we are obliged to condemn slavery, racism, economic subservience and exploitation, sexual inequality, genocide, and every other practice that destroys or degrades any person or class of persons for the aggrandizement of others. Until war and other forms of social violence are abandoned as instruments of state policy, we must grimly acknowledge that existing civilization is "cannibalistic" in its own way.

But does a thoroughgoing cultural relativism deny us the right to interpose the normative principle just stated? It does, but only when we examine the matter purely as scientists, as students of comparative anthropology, seeking to give an unbiased account of the range of accepted behaviors in the variety of human societies. Such a scientific study has its own intellectual restraints and justifications. But on the other hand if we are acting as ethical men and women attempting to understand the principles of defensible conduct in the emerging historical situation in which we live, we cannot pretend to make a virtue of such a "value-free" position as the purely descriptive sociologist is justified in assuming. (We note in passing that scientific work is never really value free, having—as indicated in a previous chapter—its own internal value system of truthfulness, fidelity to free inquiry, etc.)

To illustrate the double focus that we must maintain as scientific observers and as ethically responsible members of a living community, we observe that many a sociologist subscribing to cultural relativism in the classroom summarily abandoned his studies to enlist in the fight against the Nazis when they set out to extinguish the Jewish people. A contemporary scientist proposing to do "fieldwork" in a Nazi death camp in order, let us say, to study the sociology of genocide in contemporary society would be considered morally abominable, if not mad.

The enormity of the Nazi crime lay not solely in the fact that the Nazis committed genocide. History is replete with examples of genocide committed by most of the surviving races and ethnic communities of the world, who regrettably often look back upon the exploits of their ancestors with guiltless fascination and pride. What was horrifying and utterly unredeemable about the Nazi crime was its perpetration in the modern era—an age no longer made up of isolated island cultures whose members could convince themselves in their insulated worlds that "the stranger" belonged to a different and inferior species. The Nazis outraged and disgraced humanity because they denied a fact of contemporary life that is even now only imperfectly respected. We are members of a global species in which the various national and racial cultures are but subtypes, making the idea of "humanity" not only possible but necessary. Thus, the revulsion that we feel toward genocide, slavery, and human inequality does not refute the principle of cultural relativism. On the contrary, it confirms the validity of the principle by underscoring the emergence in the most

recent historical epoch of a culture of universal human relatedness. In our era, a relative ethics must be relative to
the whole of the human environment, which is nothing
less than the human species in its totality.

Thus, the supposed gulf between ethical relativism and
the claims of a universally binding morality disappears.
Ethical Humanism stands at this historic juncture as the
self-conscious realization of universalist ethics in a world
community. The epochal overthrow of the moral sover-
eignty of tribal or insular ethics is the fundamental trans-
formation that has occurred during the past twenty-five
centuries, although the full moral authority of this revolution is slow in being recognized. Cultural lag is nowhere
else so obvious and so tragic. It took the shock of the Nazi
outrage to reveal how profoundly interdependent the
moral relationships of the world have become. The speed
and scope of the overturn (in terms of evolutionary eras) is
nevertheless demonstrated by the persistence of a cultural
inertia that still plagues the earth with frequent relapses into
racism, aggressive nationalism, and religious chauvinism.

The persistence of tribal morality derives from its deeply
imbedded structure in custom and language. It is instructive to recall that many languages as widely separated as
Welsh and Cherokee derive the name for their own nation
from native words that translate as "the true people" or
"the real people." Even the lofty moral philosophy of Plato
and Aristotle treated Greeks as a race of beings superior
to other races in nature and rights. The Stoics and Epi-
cureans, following the lead of the Cynics, appear to have
been among the very first of the Greeks to make the ethical
breakthrough and regard all people as moral equals in a
world city "of men and gods." In Asia Minor the great Hebrew prophets had anticipated this insight in conceiving a
universal moral law of righteousness and justice, while in
India and the Far East the approximate contemporaries

of the Biblical prophets worked out their own versions of ethical universalism.

Thus, the theory of cultural relativism does not defeat the fact of an emergent humanistic ethics, which exists as a consequence of the development of a shared human identity within the global community. In the confluence of the many tribes of "strangers" of the earth, we have met "the real people" and they are "us."

The Possibility of Grounding Our Ethics in Human Experience

When people argue that ideas of right and wrong are purely matters of private, subjective feeling, and therefore not binding on any except those who happen to have similar tastes, they are taking a recklessly cavalier view of human relationships. The founders and builders of Ethical Humanism—and of all philosophies related to Humanist ethics—have believed fervently that ethical values have an objectivity that transcends private taste or arbitrary opinion. Otherwise ethics would not be possible as a guide to behavior.

But what do we mean when we assert that ethical values are objective? Such a claim at least implies that human beings share a common nature having certain needs of sufficient constancy to enable us to describe some acts as desirable or right, in terms of enhancing human welfare or as undesirable or wrong in terms of doing harm. We see such variability in individuals and cultures that it becomes difficult in practice to know with reasonable certainty just what acts will enhance human life and contribute to its growth and fulfillment. Yet, we also discover likenesses and similarities that hold for all people. We have already suggested that human interdependence is one of these constants, particularly in the early stages of life but continuing through childhood and youth into adulthood and old age. Indeed, we never outgrow the need for a social context for our lives to flourish. The exact form of these needs may change, but in some form they endure.

It would be difficult, in fact, to show that this need is absent even in hermits, or in reclusive poets and artists, or solitary mariners navigating their small craft around the globe. We may sublimate our human relationships or live vicariously in other lives and times, as the Christian anchorite went into the desert alone to relive the sufferings of a Christ he never saw except in faith; but whether in face-to-face encounter or by imagination, we live constantly in the presence of others. It is hardly far-fetched to say that the capacity for solitude is the highest achievement of a successful socialization. While there are many unhappy souls in the world who are bereft and lonely, only the wealthy in love and memory can know the riches of introspection. So even our most secret, inner lives are windows of contemplation into the spiritual fellowship of humankind.

Note carefully what this means. We cannot become actualized as individuals, secure in our own sense of selfhood, until we have first grown a strong personal identity rooted in the social matrix: the family, the school, the vocational world of work, the national and world community, and the spiritual fellowship of the common life. All of this presupposes the social character and structure of ethics. The most profound and enduring moral values are thus socially objective in the sense of being common property. They are at least objective in the sense of being intersubjective, in linking the self to other selves in a community of shared living. They may be objective in other ways as well. But at a minimum, we must recognize their reality as life-giving and life-enhancing social forces.

The series of social institutions that we have enumerated above follows the scheme of a dynamic field of widening concentric circles within which Felix Adler placed the origin and nurture of human personality. Tracing moral creativity through that series is one of the goals of this study, although we have deviated from his order by considering first of all the religious—the widest circle of the series. We have done so in order to introduce at the beginning of our inquiry the philosophical and spiritual underpinnings of our Ethical Humanist faith. We have moved in the present chapter to examine more closely the educational component in ethical growth—illustrated in the school and the theory of moral development that it expresses—although moral development has its all-important beginnings in the family and continues throughout the series. In the following chapters we shall proceed to examine the ethical life in its social and civic dimensions, looking especially at the world of productive work, and the struggle for democratic community and social justice. Finally we shall return to the more intimate spheres of living, to personal values, the place of sexuality, marriage, and family values in the Ethical Humanist way of life. Throughout all, we shall conceive the ethical life as Adler considered it, as a socially inclusive field of active, creative relationships through which human beings grow into full personhood and are thus enabled to realize the richest meanings of life.

The Concept of Character Formation: Basis of the Ethical School

Preliminary to further examination of the schools that Adler built are a few additional aspects of educational psychology that we should observe. But before touching on these, we can summarize what we have already learned of Adler's ethical philosophy by noting that he believed that an adequate ethical relationship must possess several distinguishing characteristics:

   1. It must recognize the absolute worth, the inherent value of every person, who must never be treated merely or primarily as a means to an end. Each personality must be respected as an end in itself.

2. It must affirm the uniqueness of each person, avoiding the imposition of external norms and rules of conformity that violate individuality and tend to reduce all character to a fixed mold.

3. It must be a reciprocal, or mutual, relationship, recognizing that a truly creative relationship is one that involves giving and receiving on both sides. Even the completely disabled patient needs an opportunity to give whatever he or she is able to give in return for care and kindness received, even if that ability is limited to expressing appreciation and love for love received.

4. It must enable each person in the relationship to grow into a richer and finer personality, to achieve broader and more adequate appreciations and insights as a result of the shared experience. This is summarized in the maxim: So act as to elicit the best in others and thereby in yourself.

Many practical difficulties may interfere with the optimum expression of human mutuality in our relationships. How effectively people are enabled to grow is conditioned by the degree to which disabling influences are absent or can be overcome through more helpful experiences.

First, keeping in mind Adler's stipulations as seen in the four points just summarized, we observe that an ethical act is never a completely one-sided experience, with one person passively accepting domination by another. We can return to our earlier example of the bond between mother and infant child to observe the archetypical human relationship, celebrated by artists and moralists, and endlessly probed by psychoanalysts. Even from the moment of birth, the relationship is an active and reciprocal one for both mother and child. The mother learns from the child, at the same time the child is conditioned by the mother. As a result of her unique experience, the mother becomes awakened to facets of her personality that were unknown to her before. She does not stop being the person she was before, but a new sphere of experience interacts with her prematernal self, enriching her attitudes, values, and self-image. If this change does not occur appropriately, her experience of motherhood is impaired and her child suffers also.

So also with the father: where the relationship to the child and the family is complete, the father undergoes a similar, but also uniquely distinguishable, experience making him a complementary, but different factor in the child's expanding social universe. The father, like the mother, is changed by the growing experience of the child-parent interaction.

There are a thousand variations—and as many possible interferences—in the reciprocal relationship between infant and adult. These not only affect the parent-child bond, but also pattern the moral development of the child and the adolescent in every aspect of education and character formation. It would take supernatural wisdom and skill for the affected parent to be able to shield the child from every such adverse influence.

Multiply these variables in the many relationships of a growing child's life. The child moves to a new school and is without friends or even acquaintances. The family lives into an unaccepting neighborhood where the child is shunned because of racial or cultural prejudices. A friend is domineering and imposes unfairly, or the child is molested sexually by an older neighbor. These are familiar experiences, and in one aspect or another have affected virtually all of us in growing up. The resolution and effectiveness with which we overcome such difficulties reflect an expectation about life that provides the foundation for our personality and character.

The pioneer psychotherapist, Alfred Adler (who was not related to Felix, although he became a leading member of the Vienna Ethical Society and lectured to Ethical Culture audiences in America) developed the seminal concept of "life-style," a term that unfortunately has suffered much devaluation through popular misuse. What Alfred Adler meant by life-style is the individual's characteristic way of interpreting life situations and of responding to them. A person's life-style, Adler held, becomes deeply ingrained in the first years of infancy and is resistant to change. The characteristic life-style of the emotionally secure, healthy minded person is trusting, confident, optimistic, friendly, and open. Rebuffs and injustices are easily set aside without prolonged anger and resentment. The emotionally damaged person, in contrast, has a characteristic response of suspicion, hostility, and defensiveness that colors every new experience and relationship. Such people cannot accept goodwill and genuine friendship since they are incapable of feeling generously toward others. Instead, they always look for ulterior motives.

What we see at work, therefore, is not a purely objective life situation that people meet in a completely realistic manner. Each of us brings a distinctive mind-set, a characteristic life-style, to each new relationship. As a result, every experience is colored by our expectation. Needless to say, we often trigger the response in others that we anticipate. While this situation is within the province of psychology, it has direct bearing upon the capacity for moral growth.

A notable feature of the creative ethical relationship that bears special notice is its character of openness. As Felix Adler interpreted the growth of the self, we enrich (and transform) our lives by first contributing to the creative growth of another. Like happiness, which we cannot capture by direct pursuit, moral growth within oneself is attained indirectly through the moral gift that one presents to another: the gift of becoming a richer, fuller self. To paraphrase an ancient scripture: Those who "lose" their lives for a new dimension of life shall find life more abundantly.

The openness and spontaneity of ethical experience is our answer to those who charge that the world's greatest evils are committed by people who take ethics and morality "too seriously." A bad morality is still bad, no matter how little of it one has. And a good morality (which means a creative state of human relationships) remains good, no matter how wholeheartedly one enters into it. The world's gravest cruelties and most obsessive fanaticisms result from the attitudes and actions of those who counterfeit genuine, creative morality with the false coin of hateful and rapacious "moral" tyrannies. (Consider the murderous epidemics of religious terror that periodically break out in many parts of the world.) Fanaticism is not wisdom carried to excess. On the contrary, fanaticism is moral idiocy ruthlessly expressed. In like manner, a destructively narrow, authoritarian moralism does not indicate a superabundance of moral energy, but its egotistical displacement and decay.

There can never be an excess of the moral good that expresses our growing involvement in the expanding sphere of human association and cultural interchange. Later students of creativity in ethical relationships either followed Felix Adler's lead in this recognition or independently followed the same trends in ethical theory that had set Adler on his original course.

A widely admired philosopher of religion, Henry Nelson Wieman, called this life-giving power the creative good, which, insofar as it remains always open to ever-greater creative interchange, cannot become destructive—the only power accessible to human life of which this can be said without qualification. For this reason, throughout much of his long teaching career Wieman called himself a "naturalistic theist" and identified creative interchange with God, although denying that there is anything of a supernatural character involved. He justified his radical reconception of God by arguing that creative interchange, as he described it, is the true source of human good, which earlier ages, with their limited knowledge of moral and spiritual reality, had crudely understood in terms of miracle-working divine powers. (Late in his life, it is interesting to observe, Wieman's writings do not refer to moral creativity in theological language; and he is careful to specify the ways in which creativity differs from the God concept, as well as to show parallels. At the age of eighty-nine he became an original signer of the Second Humanist Manifesto to signify his wholehearted endorsement of philosophical and religious naturalism.)

A philosopher of far greater influence than Wieman surprised many of his fellow Humanists when he tentatively proposed a somewhat similar naturalistic concept of God. In his book, *A Common Faith*, Dewey made it clear that he rejected "the God of theism" and every other suggestion of a personal or supernatural deity, but nevertheless he thought there was religious value in preserving a sense of spiritual connectedness with the favorable forces of the universe. Both militant atheism and fundamentalist Christianity have one characteristic in common: both create a wide gulf between human beings and the creative processes of the universe, which Dewey saw as deserving the religious attitude of reverence. To overcome this separation, he suggested that the word God, with its strong association with feelings of awe and worship, might be given to the creative process whereby ideal values undergo continuous correction and enlargement through experience. From this viewpoint he said, God is "the active relationship between the actual and the ideal," although he was careful to add that he did not insist on calling this process "God." Many philosophical naturalists criticized Dewey's proposal on the ground that theological language unavoidably brings to mind the traditional God of supernatural theism that Dewey explicitly rejected. Nevertheless, religious Humanists welcomed his argument that religious feeling in relation to the life-nurturing aspects of the universe is worth fostering.

The roots of the creative good go deep into our mammalian nature and evolution. (Remember that "mammal" means the animal with breasts; the animal that nurses its young.) Spiritual realization, experienced in social living, springs from our inborn capacity for empathy with other life, a consequence of being the creature that is nursed and that nurses. Those things we most cherish in life must be realized through our involvement creatively in other lives. The creative good is a self-transcending process that, not so paradoxically, supports and heightens self-appreciation and a secure individuality.

Readers who are familiar with the literature of contemporary educational philosophy will find the preceding discussion familiar. If this approach contains the germ of the religious and educational theory of Ethical Culture, as first elaborated by Felix Adler and his precursors, it has been greatly enriched by John Dewey's religious Humanism, by the psychological insights of Harry Stack Sullivan, Karen Horney, and Erich Fromm in their plumbing of the interpersonal forces that shape us, and by the many other educational psychologists and ethicists who have sought to replace magic and dogma with verifiable knowledge of how we grow.

The Ethical Culture Schools and Sunday Schools

Together with the founding of the first Ethical Culture societies, Felix Adler's greatest accomplishment was in founding the Ethical Culture Schools of New York. The continuing success of the schools after more than a century of academic distinction attests to his genius as an educational reformer and innovator. Similarly, the societies continue to demonstrate his conviction that it is possible to build a distinctive and enduring religious movement solely on the foundation of a shared ethical commitment.

As we have noted, many of the concepts of education that Adler applied had been worked out in the experimental schools of Europe, particularly in Switzerland and Germany, by such illustrious teachers as Pestalozzi and Froebel. In New England similar innovations were made by Bronson Alcott, to whom Emerson and other transcendentalist philosophers owed much, and by Emerson's friend, Elizabeth Peabody, who established the first kindergarden training school in America on Friedrich Froebel's educational model.

These departures from conventional methods replaced rote learning, which had been enforced by regimented discipline and a generous application of punishment. The classroom became a place in which the child's imagination and natural curiosity were encouraged. Moral growth was stressed along with intellectual development, as Pestalozzi had favored. Thus we see Adler's dependence as an educator on the same circle of advanced thinkers and visionaries who had also inspired in America the Free Religious Association and the rise of pronounced humanistic tendencies in the Western Unitarian Conference.

To acknowledge Adler's indebtedness to the intellectual prophets who had heralded the liberating movements of his century takes nothing away from his own unique recombination of the principles and methods that he had made his own. On the contrary, he succeeded in establishing vital, enduring institutions in the fields of education and religion, because he so creatively applied the most advanced learning of his time. He brought to his enterprise an ability to plan and coordinate, to organize, lead, and inspire; and always he was able to attract talented and dedicated people to work with him and to provide the needed financial backing. As a result, the Ethical Culture Schools that he founded in midtown Manhattan (adjoining the Society), and later at Fieldston in the Bronx, had become nationally recognized institutions long before his death in 1933.

In the more than half-century since, the schools have continued to be widely studied as models for academic excellence and commitment to ethical growth as an integral aspect of education. Their combined student bodies totaling fifteen hundred, drawn from every race, religion, social stratum, and economic class (rendered possible by a generous scholarship program) make the three schools the largest nonparochial private day-school system in the country. The overwhelming majority of the students come from families having no affiliation with Ethical Societies, although surveys of parental attitudes have shown consistent support for the nonsectarian ethical and humanistic emphasis of the curriculum. Many parents have indicated that this emphasis, together with the ethnic and cultural diversity of the student population, determined their choice of the schools for their children. The schools, like the society that sponsors them, remain convinced that a pluralistic, democratic society depends upon an education that brings together children of widely differing cultural and racial backgrounds and beliefs.

These are the same beliefs that motivate Ethical Humanists, both within and beyond the organized Ethical movement, to work for a strong public school system fitted to introduce students to a cross section of the richness and diversity of American society. This means public schools that are inclusive in spirit as well as fact, institutions that respect the plurality of beliefs—both religious and nonreligious—that exist in the American population. As we shall see in a later chapter, this concern has moved Ethical Culture members to give consistent support to the separation of church and state and to oppose as a violation of individual conscience all attempts to introduce religious indoctrination into public education.

Since most children of Ethical Culture parentage attend public schools, the openness, fairness, and religious neutrality of public education is an immediate, personal concern to the families involved. (In addition to the New York Society, only Brooklyn and Washington sponsor, or have recently sponsored, day schools of their own; in all cases these schools have not been parochial or membership-centered in design or enrollment.)

With most children of Ethical Humanist families attending the public school, responsibility for their religious education falls upon the Ethical Sunday schools that individual societies conduct. Each local fellowship or society has control over the content and management of its Sunday school, with curriculum assistance and teacher-training workshops made available by the American Ethical Union. The religious philosophy and methods of the children's program reflect those of the movement as a whole. In an American environment dominated by religious fundamentalism and sectarian exclusiveness, the Ethical Sunday school helps children to understand the principles and values of Ethical Humanism and to regard themselves as fully accepted individuals in a mutually supportive spiritual community.

Ethical nurture is contagious, muses Ethical leader and psychologist Robert Berson, and our mission is to be as infectious as possible.

CHAPTER SEVEN

Toward an Inclusive Humanist Way

As we have shown, Ethical Culture and Humanism be-gan as separate but closely related movements expressing similar moral and humanitarian values—their differences largely reflecting the personal temperaments and cultural circumstances of their founders. As these twin currents of humanistic moral commitment converged into a common spiritual community, we are not surprised to find a virtual identity in their social ideals and democratic loyalties. For both, democracy is more than just a formal political structure. It is also a moral and spiritual process of creative human interaction. Without the spirit of democracy, the life of the human community suffers stagnation, distortion, and finally, disruption. In recognizing this truth, and in basing their social ethics on the imperatives of equality and mutuality that democratic living implies, Ethical Culture and Humanism have shown their practical identity as a moral faith and way of life. Indeed, one searches in vain to discover any major differences in the social philosophy and civic conscience of these two movements, as they have developed during the century of their parallel existence.

In the opening pages of this book, I related how I dis-

covered myself in spirit to be an Ethical Culturist the summer I completed high school. No Ethical Society existed
within a thousand miles, but I soon became an avid reader
of the Ethical movement's official journal, *The Standard,*
which fortunately was available in my college library. I also
joined the American Humanist Association and corresponded with its executive director and editor, Edwin H.
Wilson, who at that time edited *The Humanist* and con-
ducted the work of the AHA from the office of the Salt
Lake City Unitarian Church, where he served as minister.
(Shortly thereafter, Wilson was able to leave the active
ministry to become the first salaried full-time director of
the AHA.)

My dual interest in Ethical Culture and Humanism was
inspired by the conviction that these two worthy and complementary expressions of humanistic idealism were right-
fully segments of a broadly conceived, inclusive Ethical
Humanist movement. My youthful hope was soon vindi-
cated by the founding in 1952 of the International Humanist and Ethical Union. Since that date the Ethical
Humanist world community has been united, a global
fellowship in which each member organization pursues its
own distinctive practices, traditions, and institutional forms.

While from time to time someone will propose a merger
of the Ethical movement and the American Humanist Association, experience has convinced most members of both
groups that the two organizations are stronger separately
than they could ever be together. They serve overlapping
but distinctive constituencies, and their organizational styles
are too different to be combined without substantial loss.
(The same can be said of Ethical Societies in contrast to
those predominately humanistic congregations within Unitarian Universalist Association; a merger would efface
Ethical Culture without substantially strengthening the
more numerous but geographically scattered Humanists
of the UUA.) Good fences not only make good neighbors

but can also conserve distinctive strengths, as each organization serves the function that it does best.

The very formulation of the term, "Ethical Humanist," to designate the common philosophy of the IHEU—as well as inclusion of both "Humanist" and "Ethical" in the name of the International body—showed awareness and sensitivity toward the distinct emphasis of the two traditions that were being joined in cooperative union. If democracy manifests the essential ethics of human community, a respect for diversity serves as its active principle, as both Felix Adler and John Dewey emphasized. The spirit of the IHEU implies both sides of the dual tradition of Ethical Culture and Humanism. What is a full and adequate philosophy of Humanism if it is not essentially ethical at its core? And what is Ethical Culture, except the practice of the moral and spiritual principle of human growth and fulfillment— the ultimate affirmation of Humanism? This common ground—indeed, this essential identity—should be even more evident and appreciated today than it was in 1952 when the IHEU came into being.

As Ethical Humanists we boast that we are bound by no creed. This is true if a "creed," in the meaning of traditional church doctrine, is assumed to distill the eternal, divinely revealed truth that a particular church body or confession claims to hold in infallible custody. But while Ethical Humanists have no creeds in the traditional usage of the term, we certainly do have summary statements that affirm the principles and ideals that serve as guidelines for the conduct of our life and labor.

Such an abstract of principles is to be found in the founding Declaration of the IHEU adopted by the delegates at the Amsterdam Congress of 1952. That manifesto can be described as providing the social and intellectual charter of global Ethical Humanism. It is a moral and philosophical creed that affirms loyalty to the ideals of human dignity, equality of rights, democracy, intellectual liberty, and social justice. It is broad enough to accommodate both the religious and secularist tendencies within the Humanist world community on a platform of tolerance, freedom, and respect for diversity. Those enemies of Ethical Humanism who impugn the philosophical and moral commitments of our faith ought to ponder the aims that the International Humanist and Ethical Union was created to serve. The founding Declaration, which has been printed in each issue of the IHEU bulletin, states in its preamble the task of our moral labor and witness:

This congress is a response to the widespread demand for an alternative to the religions which claim to be based on revelation on the one hand and the totalitarian systems on the other. The alternative offered as a third way out of the present crisis of civilization is Humanism, which is not a sect, but the outcome of a long tradition that has inspired many of the world's thinkers and creative artists, and given rise to science. Ethical Humanism unites all those who cannot any longer believe the various creeds and are willing to base their convictions on respect for man as a spiritual and moral being.

The Democratic Spirit as a Legacy of Struggle for Human Freedom

To grasp fully the impact of the words of the preamble on those who wrote them, we must recall that the delegates gathered in Amsterdam in 1952 were survivors of the struggle against Hitler's aggression, which had ended only seven years earlier. Many had served in the anti-Nazi underground Resistance and had seen their friends and families shot as hostages or sent away to die in concentration camps. Many were citizens of nations on the front line facing Stalin's aggressive totalitarianism. A reign of terror prevailed in the Soviet-occupied countries of Eastern Europe as the Kremlin dictator mercilessly snuffed out the last vestiges of democratic life in Czechoslovakia, Poland, the Baltic states, and the other subject nations. It was not at all certain that democracy could hold its ground even in Western Europe. Both Italy and France had recently faced the possibility of a seizure of power by their powerful Communist Parties. The danger had been convincingly illustrated most recently in Czechoslovakia and Hungary, where democratic governments had been crushed with the connivance of the occupying Soviet power. In this setting the IHEU delegates, with Julian Huxley serving as their honorary chair, committed themselves unequivocally for democracy, the open society, and scientific research and intellectual discussion free from ideological control.

We should not forget that Stalin's totalitarian police state had condemned to prison and death the Soviet Union's greatest biologists—some of the best in the world—for refusing to submit to the bogus "science" of Stalin's favorite, the charlatan plant breeder, Trofim Denisovich Lysenko. Huxley and his American former student and coworker, H. J. Muller—Nobel laureate and future president of the American Humanist Association—were among many Western scientists who in 1952 sounded the alarm over the totalitarian threat to intellectual freedom and the future of democracy. As a young idealist, Muller had volunteered to work in the Soviet Union as senior geneticist at the Moscow Institute of Genetics (1933–37), but as Stalin's ideological grip tightened over Soviet science and culture, Muller returned to the U.S., thoroughly awakened by his Russian sojourn to the menace of totalitarianism, whether of left or right.

In that moment of world crisis it appeared possible for democratic civilization to be erased not only from Europe, but perhaps from the world. The United States was caught up in the anti-Communist hysteria of McCarthyism, which threatened to terminate all liberalism and dissent in the name of "Americanism." In Korea, United Nations forces led by the military services of the U.S. fended off invasion from Communist North Korea and China. At this unpromising period for human freedom, the delegates at Amsterdam, assembled from North America, Western Europe, and India, adopted the five points of the IHEU Declaration that announced their unqualified loyalty to human freedom and democratic society. Altogether the five points summarize the social and intellectual commitments of Ethical Humanism:

1. It is democratic. It aims at the fullest possible development of every human being. It holds that this is a matter of right. The democratic principle can be applied to all human relationships, and is not restricted to methods of government.

2. It seeks to use science creatively, not destructively. It advocates a worldwide application of scientific method to problems of human welfare. Humanists believe that the tremendous problems with which mankind is faced in this age of transition can be solved. Science gives the means but does not propose ends.

3. Humanism is ethical. It affirms the dignity of man and the right of the individual to the greatest possible freedom of development compatible with the rights of others. There is a danger that in seeking to utilize scientific knowledge in a complex society individual freedom may be threatened by the very impersonal machine that has been created to save it. Ethical Humanism therefore rejects totalitarian attempts to perfect the machine in order to obtain immediate gains at the cost of human values.

4. It insists that personal liberty is an end that must be combined with social responsibility in order that it shall not be sacrificed to the improvement of material conditions. Without intellectual liberty, fundamental research, on which progress in the long run must depend, would not be possible. Humanism ventures to build on the free person responsible to society. On behalf of individual freedom humanism is undogmatic, imposing no creed upon its ad-

herents. It is thus committed to education free from indoctrination.

5. It is a way of life, aiming at the maximum possible fulfillment, through the cultivation of ethical and creative living. It can be a way of life for everyone everywhere if the
individual is capable of the response required by the
changing social order.

The Declaration concludes with an expression of faith
in the potential of Ethical Humanism, applying scientific
knowledge "for purposes of peace" to overcome the crisis
of civilization. "Liberated from fear," the statement closes,
"the energies of man will be available for a self-realization
to which it is impossible to see the limit. Ethical Humanism
is thus a faith that answers the challenge of our time."

The Religion of Deed That Nurtured Religious Humanism

Edwin H. Wilson, signer of the Humanist Manifesto of
1933 and coeditor with Paul Kurtz of the Second Humanist
Manifesto forty years later, at the time of this writing is
one of only three surviving signers of the earlier document.
Not only did he build the American Humanist Association
from a small, informally organized circle of religious Humanists in the early 1930s into the incorporated body that
emerged a decade later, but he also serves as a foremost
historian and walking memory bank of the organized Humanist movement in North America.

From his perspective Wilson has reiterated a point we
have made from the vantage of Ethical Culture: The fore-
runner and direct ancestor of the AHA, Wilson contends,
was the Free Religious Association. We have staked out the
same claim with respect to Ethical Culture. Adler was
counseled, supported, and inspired in collegial fellowship
by his fellow members of the FRA, especially by Frothingham. If he despaired of the association's looseness of

organization and inability to move forward, a limitation that prompted the organization of the Ethical Culture Society as a more promising alternative, Adler had no cause to complain of the record of social activism of his friends of the FRA. In the history of the Abolitionist struggle, many of the Free Religionists had played stellar roles. Their social action had often been undertaken at considerable personal risk and in defiance of federal law that mandated the surrender of runaway slaves. The militants could hardly doubt that their chief hero and exemplar in radical Abolitionism, Theodore Parker, would have been among the founders of the FRA except for his early death on the eve of the Civil War.

Before ill health had forced him to take leave from his ministry to seek a rest cure in Italy, where he died, Parker had written his greatest antislavery sermons with a loaded pistol on his desk because of serious threats to his safety. His protégé, Thomas Wentworth Higginson, the most romantic figure among the Free Religionists, hated slavery with such passion that he became a leading activist of the Boston Vigilance Committee, which aided the escape of fugitive slaves by violent means if necessary. When a fugitive, Anthony Burns, was being held in Boston's courthouse for delivery to his Southern master, Higginson bought axes and participated in an assault to demolish the courthouse doors and free the captive. Their lawless interposition, justified in the name of the higher law of human dignity and American liberty, was modeled consciously on the example of their Revolutionary grandfathers. Later, during the Civil War, Higginson resigned his commission as captain in a Massachusetts company to organize and serve as colonel of the first black regiment of the Union army.

Higginson's ministry was considered so radical on such issues as slavery, women's rights, and labor issues that he had difficulty in serving even the most liberal Unitarian congregations. When Adler's Ethical Culture appeared on the scene, Higginson compared his Free Church of Lynn (Massachusetts), which professed no Christian theology, to the Ethical Culture Society. "Natural religion," said Higginson, was sufficient without supernatural Christianity. Unlike Adler, however, Higginson wanted his church to maintain no official membership roll or other requirements and, not surprisingly, he built no movement. Nevertheless, he was a charasmatic and celebrated figure; until his death in 1911 he personified for millions the uncompromising radical prophet of racial and sexual equality and social justice—a true spiritual heir of the abolitionist Jeremiah, Theodore Parker.

The Rights of Women as the Concomitant of Racial Justice

If Higginson was the most dashing figure among the religious radicals of the FRA (although *unfortunately* one who *discounted* the importance of their being organized), Lucretia Mott, a crusading Quaker of the liberal "Hicksite" branch of the Friends, was surely the most singular in her "plain" garb, her gentle, nonviolent message stiffened by the steel backbone of her will. Few could then foresee that the Quaker preacher in their midst, who appealed for a creedless, nonsectarian piety of good deeds and liberty of conscience, was the harbinger of a cause that would become the companion movement to the struggle of the emancipated slaves for equal rights.

Repeatedly in American history, the struggle to gain freedom and legal equality for black people and to bring an end to discrimination against them and other minorities, has had the effect of "raising consciousness" about the similar plight of women. To his credit, the leader of the radical Abolitionist movement, William Lloyd Garrison, recognized this parallel at the outset of his crusade for human freedom and dignity. From the early 1830s when he undertook his work, Garrison was contemptuous of those who urged him to keep women on the back benches of the Abolitionist movement for fear of alienating conventional opinion. Garrison would have none of it, insisting that the "sisters" be given equal opportunity to speak and to lead; and his associate, Maria Weston Chapman, was one of the movement's most effective, forceful champions. To Garrison, the causes of Abolitionism, the rights of women, and "nonresistance" (radical religious pacifism) were equally sacred causes, and he refused to compromise the future of one good cause for the "practical" gain of another.

Lucretia Mott's witness for women's rights, encouraged by a handful of males (few women seem to have been present) who, like Colonel Higginson, had been won over to the feminist cause during the Abolitionist struggle, heralded a cause that has loomed ever larger in the consciousness of liberal religion and Ethical Humanism. From Free Religion in the post-Civil War decade, to Ethical Culture a decade later, and through the religiously radical "Ethical Basis" bloc of the Western Unitarian Conference to the contemporary philosophy of Ethical Humanism, the claims of the women's movement for complete equality have grown. The regrettable truth is that not all otherwise progressively minded people (including many women) have recognized the seriousness of the grievance, although great progress has been made in raising the level of consciousness in recognizing even the more subtle forms of discrimination.

When the Free Religious Association convened in those years immediately after the Civil War, Lucretia Mott could be a minister in the Religious Society of Friends, because Quakers throughout the two previous centuries of their existence had always recognized the divine calling of women to preach and to minister, on a basis of equality with men. Although Quakers had no trained or salaried clergy, they gave official recognition to those "recorded" to have ministerial gifts. As an Ethical Humanist who believes in the equality of the sexes, I am proudly descended from a woman who was recorded as a Quaker minister in Pennsylvania in the early 1700s. But if my Quaker foremother of the tenth generation before me had been an Ethical Culturist, she would have had to wait until 1903 to see Anna Garlin Spencer become the first woman accepted as an associate leader, to serve in New York with Felix Adler. At the time Ethical Culture had existed for more than a generation. Adler was clearly no Colonel Higginson on the issue of women's role in society.

The Universalists were the first American denomination with a regularly constituted professional ministry to admit a woman, Olympia Brown, who was ordained in 1863. Like Lucretia Mott, Brown became a major figure in the women's suffrage movement, and, as historian George H. Williams has noted, the only "prominent woman active in the American feminist movement from the 1860s [who] would live to see the ratification of the XIX Amendment to the Constitution in 1920," giving women the right to vote. Alas, the Free Religionists and Humanists cannot claim her! Brown was a doughty enthusiast of the bible-centered doctrine of universal salvation, the original Universalist tenet that God would eventually redeem all souls, and looked askance at the rationalism of the freethinkers who were beginning to appear in her once solidly Christian denomination. Women ministers of the Free Religionist variety would have to await the induction of women by the Unitarians a few years after Olympia Brown's reception into the ministry. One of these Unitarian women became Felix Adler's first (and only) female associate, Mrs. Spencer, the wife of a Unitarian minister who had herself served as a minister of the progressive Bell Street Chapel in Providence, Rhode Island.

Adler was slow to accept the idea of women's suffrage

or to bring a female associate into the leadership. By the time of her acceptance as an Ethical leader, Mrs. Spencer had already won acclaim among the Unitarians for her energy as a "labor preacher" who toiled among industrial workers and promoted the cause of unionism. A convinced democratic Socialist, she was an advocate of many of the progressive reforms of the era, including women's rights. To his credit, Adler recognized her merits and invited her to the New York Society as a colleague; but he had chosen a woman who was far too accomplished and energetic to be retained in a limited role, and she soon moved on to become assistant director of the New York School of Philanthrophy, which developed into the present Columbia Graduate School of Social Work.

In addition to leaving her name among the major figures of social work in America, Mrs. Spencer left the legacy of a spirited labor activist, immortalized in the hymnology of both Ethical Culture and Unitarian Universalism. Her hymn to the hero workers—set to the tune of "St. Gertrude" (familiar as the music of "Onward Christian Soldiers")—has appeared in a succession of congregational song books, extolling the virtues and victories of the heroes of labor, past, present, and future:

> Hail the hero workers
>   Of the mighty past!
> They whose labor builded
>   All the things that last.
> Thoughts of wisest meaning;
>   Deeds of noblest right;
> Patient toil in weakness;
>   Battles in the night.
>
> CHORUS: Hail, then, noble workers,
>   Builders of the past,
>   All whose lives have blest us
>   With the gains that last.

Hail ye, hero workers,
  Who today do hear
Duty's myriad voices
  Sounding high and clear;
Ye who quick responding,
  Haste ye to your task,
Be it grand or simple,
  Ye forget to ask!

CHORUS: Hail ye, noble workers,
        Builders of to-day,
        Who life's treasure gather,
        That shall last alway.

Hail ye, hero workers,
  Ye who yet shall come,
When to this world's calling
  All our lips are dumb!
Ye shall build more nobly
  If our work be true
As we pass life's treasure
  On from old to new.

CHORUS: Hail ye, then, all workers,
        Of all lands and time,
        One brave band of heroes
        With one task sublime.

The Unitarian Universalist hymn book legitimately claims Mrs. Spencer as a Unitarian, although the year of the song's composition (1907) indicates that she composed it during the decade she served as Felix Adler's associate at the New York Society for Ethical Culture. That contemporary audiences often find the sentiments of the song amusing, if not hopelessly naive and idealistic, only indicates how far progressively minded Americans have diverged from the prolabor, moderately socialistic temper that prevailed in liberal religious and progressive circles at the turn of the century. The Socialist Party, with Eugene

V. Debs as its candidate, had made rapid gains in recent presidential contests when Mrs. Spencer wrote her paean to labor. Five years later Debs would receive nearly a million votes—the highest percentage of the electorate for a socialist candidate in American history. Mrs. Spencer's prolabor and Socialist convictions were shared by several other prominent leaders of the Ethical movement, including Henry Neumann in Brooklyn, Henry Moskowitz at the Down-Town Ethical Society, and in St. Louis the recent English immigrant, Percival Chubb—of the original fourteen friends in Britain who had organized a group dedicated to human betterment that developed into the socialistic Fabian Society. Adler was prolabor and an advocate of industrial reform, but a critic of socialism, especially of the orthodox Marxist variety which, he predicted, would lead to a tyrannical centralization of power.

Why was Adler, the innovator and trailblazer in so many areas of social and educational reform, so cautious—if not actually resistant—in promoting the entrance of women into religious leadership and comparable positions? That he was not a stereotypical exponent of male dominance is clear in his writings. While there is room for more than one interpretation of his motives, two primary factors appear to have contributed to his caution; the first was traditional and absorbed from his cultural heritage, the second resulted from a misplaced application of his ethical doctrine of the uniqueness of persons and types, the enriching dissimilarities that he prized in unlike individuals, cultures, and—in this case—the sexes. The doctrine of uniqueness lead him to value and maximize unlike potentialities, affirming the distinct excellencies of each individual and type. He extolled differences of many qualities, believing, for example, that ethnic and national traits existed and that they should be welcomed as valuable and mutually fructifying—the basis of the creative social pluralism that he championed. But while this stance was valuable as an an-

tidote to the imperialistic type of assimiliationism that
sought to reduce minorities to carbon copies of the dominant Anglo-Saxon culture—à la the "melting pot"—there
is the ever-present danger that a theory of distinct human
types, whether national or sexual, can be misconstrued to
justify the discriminations and exclusions that Adler consciously deplored and combated. He strenuously argued,
and no doubt sincerely believed, that his concept of the
unique spiritual gifts and special "vocation" of women as
mothers and teachers of the race enhanced their human
dignity and ethical relationships. But he was not sufficiently
alert to the consequent restriction of the freedom of women
to choose other interests and pursuits that men had monopolized for themselves. The judgment of recent social
history has been against Adler's division of ideal sexual
roles in society.

The other principal reason for Adler's hesitation is
clearly derived from his strong conception of the traditional
family, interpreted in the familiar pattern of middle-class
European Jewish culture. Woman had held a high place
throughout Jewish history. Motherhood was honored as
the very axis around which the spiritual life of the family
rotated and expanded into the larger community. But like
many other cultures cradled in the folkways of old and
settled civilizations, women were frequently segregated,
when not altogether excluded, from public religious celebration and authority. The rabbinate was strictly a male
preserve with no analogue to the woman Quaker preacher
or the Methodist prohibitionist lecturer of the American
landscape—precedents of female assertiveness that spilled
over into women's political activism and civil disobedience.

There was also no analogue in the orderly, male-
dominated families of Europe to the boisterous make-do
existence of the American settlement, where men were
foot-loose and often absent, and independent-minded
women introduced and cultivated whatever degree of

"book-learning" and religious life was available in the continental wilderness. American women may have been slow in reaping the reward for their resourcefulness and social leadership, but from the half-Indian wife who walked the mountain trails with her fur-trading husband to the wife-mother of the wilderness farm family, the American pioneer woman has been rail-splitter, plow hand, cotton chopper, house builder, and often shouldered her own rifle—not to mention bearing her babies, caring for her young, and occasionally retrieving her stupified man from the crossroads tavern.

While today's city-bred American may be inclined to dismiss this frontier past as overly romanticized, once we venture a few miles into the continent's flanks, away from the coastal tides of European urbanity, the characters of Americans as diverse as Lincoln, Annie Oakley, Mark Twain, Dorothea Dix, Will Rogers, Jane Addams, and Martin Luther King show the stamp of a native cultural ethos substantially molded and transmitted by self-reliant, resourceful, determined women.

The Struggle for Sexual Equality in Ethical Humanist Leadership

Fifty-seven years after Anna Garlin Spencer was admitted as an associate leader in New York, Barbara Raines was certified as associate leader of the West Coast Council for Ethical Culture, and afterward served as leader of societies in California and New York state—the first woman to attain the rank of full leader. For more than a decade, Dr. Raines stood valiantly alone as a representative of her sex in the AEU leadership, always intrepid in her determination to break the barriers that women faced in entering and pursuing on equal terms a career in the professions. Ethical leadership, she felt, was not as open to women as it should be. The revival in the 1960s of the feminist movement, which had remained quiescent during the decades following passage of the XIX Amendment giving women the right to vote, added force to Dr. Raines's insistence that Ethical Humanism face its flawed record with respect to women's equal rights.

The 1970s brought swift change with many more women added to the boards of local societies and the AEU. Women leaders were added to the membership of the National Leaders' Council. It changed its name (at least in part) to overcome the sexist connotation of the previous title, the Fraternity of Leaders. The 1980s saw the election of the first woman president of the AEU National Leaders Council, Judith Espenschied.

Among the new women leaders to be added to the roster was the executive director of the AEU, Jean Somerville Kotkin. While performing the administrative duties of her demanding office, she also pursued the graduate studies in religion and counseling that equipped her professionally for certification as a leader. She became in this period one of the best known and most forceful advocates of Ethical Humanism in the Humanist world as well as the foremost organizer of new Ethical fellowships.

The younger women leaders of today and the future, whose abilities and commitment are already making it apparent that they will be major contributors to the movement's material and spiritual development, owe much to the perseverance and courage of such able leaders as these and to Mrs. Spencer's pioneering example before them. The movement as a whole, and its male members and leaders in particular, are in debt to this small group of women who overcame mind-sets and preconceptions that may have been more unintended than deliberate but which, while permitted to continue, compromised Ethical Humanism's message and belied its profession of holding all human beings in equal esteem.

As in many other religious organizations, the lay women

of Ethical Humanism offered the hearts, hands, and back-
bones that enabled groups from the smallest fellowship to
the richest and largest society to develop and to do their
work. Long before women held any of the lay offices in
the societies or were present in more than token numbers
on the governing boards of societies, schools, or service
organizations, they were the first to be turned to for volunteer work—and the last to despair when societies were
in trouble and required added drudgery and resourcefulness to survive. More often than not, they were the
healers in crises of conflict. In many of these times of trib-
ulation or decline, the chapters of the National Women's
Conference (now the National Service Conference, which
recently admitted men to their membership) have kept local
groups alive and led their recovery.

Among the lay leadership and offices of the AUE and
its member societies, women have rapidly become prominent in greater numbers. To its credit, the American Ethical Union elected its first woman president more than sixty
years prior to the writing of this account. Mrs. Martha Fi-
schel of the St. Louis Society, an outstanding champion of
racial and social justice in her region, took the president's
gavel in the movement's fiftieth anniversary year. It was a
notable distinction for the AEU, which, in elevating a
woman to the post of national president in 1926, must occupy an exceptional place in the chronicles of American
religious bodies. The step is even more impressive when
we consider that for most of the prior half-century, Adler,
as founder of the movement, had occupied the presidency
as a matter of course.

During the first century of the Ethical movement, Flor-
ence Wolff Klaber, daughter of Adler's closest friend,
Alfred Wolff, became the driving force in promoting and
guiding the Children's Sunday Assembly (Sunday School)
both in the New York Society and throughout the move-

ment. An articulate and ebullient teacher, Mrs. Klaber combined the skills of an administrator with the creative ability of a skilled storyteller and writer. When the Beacon Press, the publishing house of the American Unitarian Association, in the mid-twentieth century undertook development of a new religious education curriculum for children, to be based on contemporary psychological insights and religious scholarship, Mrs. Klaber was invited to serve on the curriculum committee and to be one of the writers of the children's books and teachers' guides.

The New Beacon Curriculum won immediate recognition from leading "mainline" religious educators for its effective, nondogmatic methods and content; and it long served as a model curriculum for the major denominations. Used widely by Ethical Culture and by Unitarian and Universalist Sunday Schools (as well as by many liberal Congregationalist church schools), Mrs. Klaber's books instructed more children and their teachers than there were probably readers for all the other AEU publications and leaders' addresses combined! If anyone had ever thought of telling her that she had become the movement's most widely studied author and teacher (for Mrs. Klaber was far too self-effacing to entertain such a thought herself), she would have tossed her head and laughed.

Despite changing economic and cultural patterns in American life—plus the fact that today's Ethical member is less likely to belong to the wealthy elite than was once the case—today's women in Ethical Culture bear a disproportionate share of the load for volunteer community services and programs to support world peace and international understanding. But in the years since World War II, women have played an increasing role of leadership in conceiving and shaping programs, where once they would have likely played supportive but subordinate parts.

When in 1946 the Ethical movement undertook establishment of summer camps to bring together young people of different racial, national, and cultural backgrounds to study and practice democratic living in a totally interracial setting, a program that became internationally prominent as the Encampment for Citizenship, a lay member of the New York Society, Alice K. Politzer, joined her vision and energy to that of Ethical leaders Algernon D. Black and Henry B. Herman to create the program. Her efforts promoted the Encampment's development for the following thirty years. In a similar act of moral commitment, a group of Ethical Culture women of the New York City area, organized by May Weiss of the New York Society, created and staffed as volunteers the United Nations office of the International Humanist and Ethical Union, a member office of the United Nation's officially recognized nongovernmental Organizations. Rebecca Goldblum, who served in many capacities in the AEU and the National Women's Conference of the AEU, sparked movementwide efforts in support of abortion rights reform. As an Executive Committee member and Vice President of the AEU, she was tireless in her determination to make the Ethical Humanist movement aware of the social and legal plight of women, both in the United States and abroad, and to become involved in the struggle for equality. She was equally active in support of the First Amendment principle of church-state separation and support of public education free from religious indoctrination. Only their deaths after long and productive lives of service, terminated the undefatigible enthusiasm—but not the influence—of these three exceptional Ethical Humanists.

Many other women have made noteworthy contributions to the humanitarian labors, educational work, and social witness of the Ethical Humanist movement's first century. If this were a systematic history, rather than a mere glimpse into the life and spirit of Ethical Humanism, we would require many additional pages to sketch their stories.

(An account of the more prominent figures of the earlier segment of this history can be found in Howard Radest's excellent general history of Ethical Culture's first seventy-five years, *Toward Common Ground,* Frederick Ungar Publishing Co., New York. 1969.)

CHAPTER EIGHT

Social Conscience and the Ideal of Ethical Democracy

The social heritage of today's Ethical Humanism proceeds from a blending of the two philosophical currents that we have traced through the minds of Felix Adler and John Dewey. Although Adler was only eight years Dewey's senior, the precociousness and educational advantages of the former enabled him to become a widely recognized figure in religion, education, and social reform before Dewey could become established in his career as a college teacher. A farm boy from Vermont, who taught school before enrolling at Johns Hopkins University for his doctoral studies, Dewey received his Ph.D. in 1884. He began teaching in 1888 at the University of Minnesota, and the following year moved to the University of Michigan. At Chicago in 1894 he undertook the educational research that made him famous, pioneering new methods of child-centered teaching at the University's Laboratory School. He then moved to Columbia University where he taught for the remainder of his long career in philosophy and education.

Dewey has since been blamed by a misinformed public, seriously misled by propagandists of the ideological right wing, of having initiated the decline of intellectual rigor in American public education—a curious charge against a thinker who insisted that the classroom should be a working laboratory where scientific methods and disciplines are learned through firsthand application. The real motivation for attacking Dewey is not to correct his alleged intellectual laxness, but to discredit his opposition to the authoritarian practices used to instill rote learning and indoctrination. As the classroom becomes a laboratory, said Dewey, so should it exemplify the spirit of the democratic community. What is more "democratic"—in the sense of being open and accessible to all—than the scientific method? What are more contrary to the authoritarian, vested interests and structures of society than the self-critical, question-raising processes of science and democratic living?

The enemies of contemporary liberal education and humanistic philosophy are on the mark only in choosing Dewey as their chief devil. For he soon outranked all his competition as a democratic theorist and educator of national significance. Few philosophers in any age have had a greater impact on their times. Dewey was also a writer of influential magazine articles, especially in *The New Republic,* at a time when many Americans were debating the future of capitalism and questioning the relevance of liberal constitutional government. He participated in committees for political reform, the rights of unions, industrial democracy, and academic freedom, serving as the first president of the American Association of University Professors, which he had helped bring into being.

After the deaths early in the century of William James and Charles S. Peirce, Dewey had no peer. He remained without challenge *the* American philosopher for the forty years preceding his death in 1952 at the age of ninety-three. Since his time no American philosopher has even come close in matching his fame or influence. He was—and still is—recognized worldwide as the philosopher of democracy, par excellence. Twice he journeyed to China to teach and was invited to Turkey by Ataturk's revolutionary government to offer expert guidance on the reorganization of the Turkish school system according to modern, secular principles of education. When Franklin Roosevelt's New Deal was introducing new conceptions of government's role in industrial relations and economic planning, Dewey was a familiar figure among the theoreticians of democratic cooperation and community action.

To Felix Adler and his version of democratic social idealism, Dewey's influence was not entirely welcome. Even Adler's closest and most appreciative students and biographers have suggested that professional pride as an educational innovator may have made it difficult for Adler to give full credit to the educational and philosophical accomplishments of his younger "rival." (It is said by those who knew both men well that Dewey did not return Adler's feeling of competitiveness, but always responded with generous recognition of Adler's educational and social contributions.)

The Ethical Humanist movement owes to Adler its institutional forms, its organized spiritual communities, its many applied social services and community agencies, and its strong commitment to a sense of ethical mission. But as a thinker and teacher of the first magnitude, whose philosophical stature places him among the greatest of the centuries, Dewey had no match in Adler or any other American contemporary. Yet, both the likenesses and differences of these two humanistic innovators make impressive lists.

Among their likenesses: A passionate commitment to the fundamental value of the person; unqualified loyalty to the democratic process; a belief that democracy is in essence an ethical concept that applies broadly to all social structures and relationships; a commitment to social reform to actualize the human potential within each of society's members; devotion to intellectual freedom and the unfettered use of the rational mind ("intelligence," in Dewey's language) to secure reliable moral knowledge as a guide to action; belief in racial equality and social justice; concern for world peace and support for the development of international covenants and organizations to prevent war; opposition to the imperialism of the "advanced" nations over the less developed; opposition to thought control and to totalitarian methods, whether of the left or the right; the conviction that social and economic competition must be limited and cooperative industrial organization advanced through democratic means; the belief that the organization of the classroom should serve as a demonstration of democracy, and that the school should function as a workshop and laboratory where children can directly experience and internalize skills, knowledge, and values; the belief that education is a lifelong process that is coextensive with the whole of democratic labor and community, so that school, industry, and society interface and interact.

Even this list is far from exhaustive in specifying the concepts and ideals that Adler and Dewey shared. While there were inevitably nuances, shades of difference, in their individual interpretation of the values and principles listed above, the social and educational ideals of both philosophers closely coincided at virtually every major point. Historians of the philosophy of education have remarked on how similar the teaching applications and methods are of ethical idealism, as developed by Adler, and of pragmatic Humanism, as elucidated by Dewey.

Their unlikenesses, as already suggested, were in part matters of personal temperamant and in part differences of intellectual background and philosophical style—Kant influencing Adler, and Hegel lingering—at least in spectral outline—in Dewey's evolutionism, even after he had abandoned Hegel for the pragmatic philosophy of Peirce and James (particularly the former) and the scientific naturalism of Darwin. Both Adler and Dewey retained more than a trace of Emerson's American optimism. They differed most sharply in their divergent conception of the nature of ideas and of how moral knowledge is theoretically grounded. Dewey abandoned entirely the classical notion, honored in philosophy from at least the time of Plato and reintroduced in modified form by Kant, that truth is transcendental in nature. For Dewey there is nothing eternal or transcendental about truth, whether "scientific" truth or "moral" truth. Ideas are instrumental. Just as surely as stone axes and cyclotrons are tools designed for striking physical objects, ideas are tools of human thought for testing experience.

For Dewey facts and values are not so different as traditional philosophy makes them appear. Truth pertains to the realm of experience and is accessible to all who investigate it by methods that are comparable to the means we use to explore the world of physical nature. Moral and ethical principles are not essentially different from other scientific principles, except that they apply to human behaviors of a particularly complex nature. But except for their specialized application, moral generalizations are like other scientific statements. They are predictions of the probable effects of particular behaviors; and they are propositional in form, telling us in effect that if we desire certain ends, such as to live harmoniously with our fellow beings, certain behaviors will carry us toward our aim while certain other behaviors will lead to conflict and disaster.

Determining which aims are life enhancing and which are not is a matter of intelligent appraisal of human experience, socially through history, and individually in personal interaction with our fellows. Dewey, of course, did not underestimate the degree to which we depend upon wisdom accumulated through trial and error by our ancestors. Ethical knowledge undergoes development and testing in the light of human needs and changing circumstances. But without moral commitment to the supreme worth and dignity of the person as our first principle of ethics, we would lack the secure foundation upon which to build our philosophy and faith of humanistic life affirmation.

The Melding of Adler's and Dewey's Thought into Ethical Humanism

The work of blending the compatible and generally complementary elements of the ethical philosophies of Adler and Dewey fell to a small group of Ethical thinkers and leaders who came upon the scene in the 1930s and 1940s. While a number of outstanding contributors to the thought of contemporary Ethical Humanism would deserve examination in a definitive study, we must content ourselves with mention of a few of the most prominent. This small circle of philosophers, educators, and professional leaders associated with Ethical Culture was a remarkably able group. They would have been outstanding in an organization many times the size of the Ethical movement. For such a small body to command the devotion of such capable intellectual leadership is a tribute to the spiritual ideal that attracted them.

The leading representatives of the group included V. T. Thayer at the schools, soon to be joined at the New York Society by two young leaders, Algernon D. Black (certified as an Ethical leader in 1934) and Jerome Nathanson (certified in 1940), and by their still younger colleague, James F. Hornback (1947), who after beginning his leadership at the New York and Westchester societies, carried the Humanist philosophy to St. Louis with his appointment there in 1951. Although Matthew Ies Spetter did not arrive on the American Ethical leadership scene until after the 1940s, he deserves mention among the innovators of the new Ethical Humanism for his earlier experience in Europe and for introducing into the American movement the type of Humanist sensibility that had developed among the Dutch

Humanists in the aftermath of World War II. Spetter had served in the underground, was captured and sent to a concentration camp, and—thanks to the war's timely end— narrowly escaped execution by the Nazis. His experience gave special passion to his commitment to democracy and his tireless labor for a religious Humanism that succors the pains and hungers of the heart as well as the needs of the intellect.

While these younger leaders developed the Ethical Humanist philosophy that emerged in the twenty years following Adler's death, the older generation of leadership continued essentially in his tradition. John L. Elliott, nationally esteemed in the world of social work and community development for his lifelong development of the Hudson Guild Settlement House and its affiliated services, had been Adler's associate in the leadership since 1894. It now fell on Elliott to assume Adler's many roles including the senior leadership of the New York Society, the rectorship of the Ethical Culture schools, and the chair of the national leadership group, the Fraternity of Leaders. He continued as the acknowledged head of the Ethical leadership until his death in 1942. David S. Muzzey at Westchester, who succeeded to the New York senior leadership following Elliott, and Henry Neumann in Brooklyn, were outstanding leaders of the old Adlerian circle—although Neumann, was a mediating figure between the original ethical idealist philosophy and the emerging naturalistic Humanism. In the Chicago Society the transition to an explicit religion of Humanism came with the appointment of A. Eustace Haydon, as mentioned earlier, a signer of the Humanist Manifesto of 1933.

These talented and forceful professionals were supplemented in scholarship and philosophical prowess by Horace L. Friess, whom we introduced earlier as Adler's son-in-law and biographer. Friess pursued an academic career at Columbia University, where he taught philosophy and religion from 1919 until his retirement in 1966. Although his primary career was in academia, his contribution to the movement was recognized by his election to the Fraternity of Leaders in 1942, and he later served for many years on the Board of Leaders in New York. A reflective writer and thinker, he was respected widely in the academic world and was beloved by a generation of leaders-in-training who were the beneficiaries of his patient counsel and unwavering encouragement. Lester Mondale, a colleague in the leadership, described Friess as "one of the Earth's noblemen." Surely he was that, and one of religious Humanism's unheralded saints. Despite his profound veneration for Adler as a person and as a spiritual genius, Friess belonged to the camp of those philosophically indebted to Dewey's Humanism. He contributed especially to deepening the religious quality of Ethical Humanism.

Foremost among the philosophical shapers of the post-Adlerian movement who were already in place when Adler died was the Director of the Ethical Culture Schools, V. T. Thayer. He had also been elected to the leadership in recognition of his philosophical stature and importance to the movement as a whole. When Adler died in 1933, Thayer was the one major figure in the Ethical Culture movement already clearly identified with the rising tide of Dewey's thought in American philosophy and education. That Adler had chosen Thayer in 1928 to head the schools is itself a tribute to Thayer's tact and ability and Adler's perspicacity in recognizing an educator and social philosopher of promise. For fifty years Adler had been one of the most innovative and imitated educational pioneers in the United States, a role that Thayer would duplicate for more than a generation to come.

When about 1950 I was attending a small Southern university preparing for a career in secondary school teaching, the name of V. T. Thayer was prominent in bibliographies of required reading on the philosophy of education and

teaching methods. (Only years later did I discover that
Thayer was associated with Ethical Culture and get to know
him during his retirement in northern Virginia.) His book,
The Passing of the Recitation, was a classic treatment of the
newer child-centered education, which had principally
emerged from the experimental work of Dewey, but also
from Adler and other distinguished educational reformers
who were rather uncritically lumped together in the public
mind as "progressive educators."

Thayer belonged to that incorruptible core of progressives who never sacrificed intellectual excellence for either
"freedom" or "democracy" in the classroom. He was sufficiently clear-headed and educationally rigorous to understand that freedom and democracy are the outcomes
as well as the necessary conditions of a classroom experience focused on the aims of ongoing learning and knowing.
Anarchy is not freedom, and chaos is not experiment or
research in any meaningful sense. Adler and Dewey
understood this well, despite the misconceptions of some
popularizers of "progressive" methods who, at their worst,
tended to reduce the classroom to self-centered preoccu-
pations and aimless play.

The reader may ask why we are covering this ground
here, rather than in the previous chapter on the ethical
schools. Our present interest concentrates on the ethical
conception of democracy and the role of social conscience,
topics that are inseparable from the principles of personal
growth and the social dynamics of community living.
Therefore, it is no accident that Ethical Humanism's greatest social philosophers have also been educators and students of moral development. Our attention must shuttle
back and forth between the complementary perspectives
of "school" and "society" if we are to understand our topic
holistically and developmentally. School and democratic
community constitute a continuum—a reality that is vio-
lated by educational formalists and "traditionalists" who,

if you stop to consider the matter, venerate the petrified artifacts of "tradition" at the cost of the dynamic processes of a living historical community.

As a philosopher of democratic life, Thayer remained true to a principle that was central to the thought of both of his immediate teachers, Adler and Dewey. Both recognized and prized the free interplay of diverse personalities and social forces in society. In a word, both were democratic pluralists, but both understood that pluralism to be genuinely pluralistic must involve free association and genuine interchange. Since both Adler and Dewey have been misunderstood on this point, their positions must be clarified.

Adler is sometimes denigrated by those having only a superficial knowledge of his thought as an "assimilationist," with the negative ideas of "melting-pot" cultural conformity that that term connotes. Did he not leave the rabbinate to found a movement that repudiated the particularistic loyalties of his ethnic community for an ethical and religious universalism that effaced differences? What else did the "common ground" of Ethical Culture imply? Adler's ethical universalism was the crowning glory of an idealism that affirmed a common human identity and the equal and reciprocal worth of all people. But, as we have emphasized throughout, the equal worth of human beings implies (as Adler was tireless in insisting) reciprocity. It is the meeting and interacting of differences that animates and invigorates the whole, enriching the personalities of each individual in an active relationship. Adler applied this to cultures and nations as well as to personal relations. Two dangers to genuine human interchange are to be avoided: the violation of the other party (person or group) by imposing the dominant party's characteristics and values—the cultural imperialism that the melting-pot concept of assimiliationism involved; and, secondly, the opposite danger of the isolation that cultural exclusion and particularism produce.

Segregation may be forced on a group, or it may be self-chosen. In either case, it produces a ghetto mentality with the inevitable prejudices that such a state involves, and diminishes human community.

Voicing his concern for the future of open, pluralistic community, Thayer broke the silence of his retirement to urge that the Ethical Culture schools avoid the excesses of particularism that were touted as "pluralism" during a period of enthusiasm for ethnicity in the late 1960s. His appeal is of lasting value to a movement based on the ideals of Ethical Humanism. Thayer recognized that a homogeneous American society is neither possible nor desirable. Adler had recognized that ninety years earlier. The Ethical Society itself represents an experiment in spiritual fellowship based upon unity in diversity, with the varied backgrounds of its members viewed as a source of mutual enrichment. The Ethical Culture schools are designed to carry that principle to a wider public and to new generations.

Thayer drew upon this experience and moral principle to urge that the excesses of both separatism and assimilationism be avoided. The school community, like the democratic society ethically conceived, is neither a melting pot nor a balkanized conglomerate of ghettos. Jews, Protestants, Catholics, atheists, blacks, whites, orientals, individuals from every ethnic, cultural, and economic background are there to give and to receive. In Adler's terms, they cannot achieve their fullest ethical potential without "repercussion," by which Adler meant the unique sense of life coming from those different from themselves.

An ethical concept of democracy, Thayer argued in terms that would have satisfied Dewey and Adler alike, "differs from excessive expressions of individualism or the submerging of individuality within a group discipline." It also avoids "competition and rivalry as between cultural groups, or a philosophy which would erase group distinctiveness, or a society of multiple groups." Thayer noted that earlier Adler and his associates had to fight against discrimination that kept minorities apart from the mainstream, even as they resisted forces that sought to erase the distinctiveness of particular minority groups. Now, he noted, we seemed to have entered a period in which new errors were being made in the name of pluralism itself.

> The assumption is that it is a primary and self-sufficient responsibility to confirm and reinforce rather than to refine and modify cultural differences and loyalties. . . . This is altogether different from the attempt to develop at one and the same time a sympathetic understanding of the differences and the origins of others, and an essential self-respect and acceptance of one's own ancestry. . . . It follows that a school that does no more than confirm an Indian or Mexican in his native culture, a Jew in his Jewishness, an Irishman in his Irishness, or a Negro in his Blackness, has failed in its primary obligation to American democracy.

The viability and coherence of American democracy rests upon our ability to understand and respond adequately to the pluralistic, interactive "ethical conception of democracy," for which Thayer so eloquently argued.

Respect for Dissenting Conscience, A Fundamental of Democracy

Writing to a group of Connecticut Baptists, a religious minority that had recently suffered severe repression in New England, Thomas Jefferson coined a phrase that has become one of the most debated in American constitutional history. Our third president declared himself resoundingly in support of the Danbury, Connecticut, dissenting Baptists and all other persecuted minorities. He spoke of "a wall of separation between church and state" as expressing the proper relationship between religion and government in a nation that prizes liberty. In much the same vein, Jefferson's understudy and presidential successor, James Madison, wrote in defense of "a line of separation between the rights of religion and the civil authority."

Madison argued that in exchange for surrendering legal recognition and financial support, religion stands to gain greater security and freedom. The religious conscience thus enjoys immunity from intrusions by civil authority, a security that does not exist where the state presumes to regulate religious belief and practice. A pastor of the Church of Sweden discovered this fact of life some years ago when he was held to be in violation of the law for refusing to officiate at a wedding for a couple whose relationship he questioned. As a civil official, he was told by the Swedish court, he had a legal obligation to solemnize the marriage whether he approved or not. What chance would such an agent of the state have in criticizing even the most morally outrageous behavior of his government?

In contrast, when the liberal minister of The First Baptist Church of Washington, D.C., criticized as a violation of the First Amendment plans of the Truman administration to appoint an ambassador to the Vatican, the church's most celebrated member, Harry Truman, stalked out in a huff, never to return. But Dr. Pruden continued to lead the voices of protest that rose from thousands of American pulpits. Madison could have told Mr. Truman why. Later, more than one indignant but powerless president has had to endure a lecture from the pulpit on the wrongness of his policy in Southeast Asia or Central America. Some Americans without a background in the thinking of the founders or the principles of constitutional law, misconstrue the First Amendment to mean that religious leaders and groups should remain silent on public issues. But, as the above situations have shown, the contrary is true. The separation of church and state enables an independent, voluntary association of believers of any faith to practice religion in their own way and criticize society, including the government, to their hearts content. In the American system, churches and clergy are free to criticize without official hindrance. They are accountable only to their membership, subject to such civil law as applies to all citizens and comparable groups.

Ethical Humanists have a special interest in freedom of religion, defined in the comprehensive terms that Madison and Jefferson understood that freedom to embrace. Conceptions of religion that narrow the constitutional application of the First Amendment or that weaken the ban on government interference or preferment are of particular concern to a religious philosophy that is committed to freedom of conscience and abhors theological tests or requirements of any kind.

Ethical Humanists and other religious liberals and nonconformists have had to resist persistent pressures in American society to narrow the First Amendment to mean—as the popular cliché phrases it—"freedom to worship God." The Constitution does not mention God or worship, either in its original body or in any of its amendments. Even the words, "so help you God," conventionally added to swearing-in ceremonies, do not appear in the oath that the Constitution prescribes for office holders. On the contrary, the only mention of religion in the Constitution as originally ratified was negative: No religious test shall ever be required of Federal office holders. The equal-protection clause of the Fourteenth Amendment, ratified shortly after the Civil War, extends that constitutional prohibition to the states.

The Constitution and its Amendments do not specify "worship" in protecting religion. To limit the meaning of religious freedom to freedom of worship—whether the worship of God or of any other religious object—is clearly to diminish a freedom that the constitutional framers intended to have a much more inclusive application. The First Amendment—which was introduced into the hopper of the House of Representatives during its first session by James Madison—was skillfully drafted to protect religion in all its varieties, but also to protect the citizen from any unwanted coercion in favor of religion. (Those who glibly claim that the Amendment protects freedom of religion, but not freedom *from* religion, should read more carefully.) The wording of the provision is explicit and unequivocal:

> Congress shall make no law respecting an establishment of religion, or prohibiting the free exercise thereof.

Ethical Humanists who regard their moral faith as a religion have been found by the courts to be protected in their belief, just as are persons of other religious beliefs. Atheists and others who do not consider their beliefs to be religious are also secured against unwanted religious coercion (or involuntary indoctrination). As Justice Hugo Black was fond of saying, "No law means no law!"—an apt retort to those who attempt to weaken the prohibition on "laws respecting an establishment of religion" by subtle and devious subterfuges.

The American Ethical Union was active, especially during the 1950s and 1960s when these issues were tested in the courts, in defending the legal religious status of its member societies and in supporting the rights of individuals denied equal rights of conscience by reason of their nontheistic belief. The latter group of cases included the right of individuals to qualify for state offices without theological tests (striking down a Maryland law that required belief in a Supreme Being and a future state of rewards and punishments—in effect, belief in heaven and hell—as a qualification for public office); and under Selective Service law (the military draft), the right of nontheistic conscientious objectors to receive the same treatment as other religious objectors.

Roy Torcaso, the Maryland resident referred to in the

case mentioned above, was a member of the Board of Trustees of the Washington (D.C.) Ethical Society when his landmark case was decided unanimously in his favor by the Supreme Court in 1961. Only a few years earlier the Washington society itself had won a decision in the Federal Circuit Court upholding its right to exist as a tax-exempt religious organization, a right that had been denied to it by the District of Columbia tax commissioner on the ground that an organization must require belief in God in order to qualify as a religion. In a decision written by Chief Judge Warren Burger (later the Chief Justice of the United States), the appeals court decided in the society's favor, Judge Burger noting that the Washington Ethical Society functioned as a religion in the lives of its members and that to deny religious status to such a body on doctrinal grounds would raise serious constitutional questions. As members of the AEU Law Committee and their attorneys commented later, the stakes involved in the case were far higher than the payment of taxes on a modest meeting house. (Bringing the case cost far more than many years of future taxes.) The real issue was the principle of the equal protection of rights of conscience for nontheists. This would be shown during the 1960s in a series of critical cases affecting conscientious objectors of nontheistic religious belief, an issue in which I became deeply involved as the professional leader and representative of the Ethical movement in the nation's capital.

During this period, I was called upon from time to time to represent the Ethical movement in testimony before committees of the House and Senate on questions affecting religious freedom and other human rights. Civil rights, civil liberties, the separation of church and state, and the treatment of nontheistic conscientious objectors (who were excluded under a provision of the 1948 Selective Service Act) were concerns on which I most often testified.

Although the majority of Ethical Humanists are not conscientiously opposed to participation in all war (the standing definition of legally recognized conscientious objection), a decided minority of our members, and others of similar belief, are firmly committed to nonviolence and nonparticipation in war as a deeply held ethical and religious conviction. As the frequently designated spokesperson for the Ethical movement on Capitol Hill, I was determined to do what could be done to end the unfair and unequal treatment of nontheistic conscientious objectors. After my testimony before the Senate Armed Services Committee in the spring of 1967, during which I was extensively questioned by Chairman Richard B. Russell, Senator Sam Ervin, and other members of the panel, the requirement of belief in a Supreme Being was dropped in reenacting the law.

To my great satisfaction, Senator Russell defended the proposed change on the floor of the Senate, citing constitutional principle as his reason. I had been informed in advance by the chief of staff of Russell's committee that the senator would take this position, and learned from the same source that my testimony had been the decisive factor in persuading Russell and his colleagues of the justice of the case. (My prepared statement on behalf of the American Ethical Union, together with the extensive questioning of my arguments by the Senate panel fills twenty pages of the official Hearings, remaining a primary source for those wishing to research the struggle to obtain for nontheistic COs the same legal alternative provided for those of traditional belief. [*See* Hearings Before the Committee on Armed Services, United States Senate, on S. 1432, April 12–19, 1967. U.S. Government Printing Office, *reprinted in the Appendix of this volume.*]

Not only was this victory in repealing a shamefully discriminatory provision of law gratifying to all Ethical Humanists, whether pacifist or nonpacifist, but it also brought an invitation for me and other religious representatives to meet with the director of Selective Service to respond to newly proposed regulations more in accord with the revised law and recent Supreme Court decisions that broadened the meaning of religion. Ultimately the director accepted my suggestion that instead of writing new definitions of their own, Selective Service simply adopt the Supreme Court's formula accepting "ethical beliefs," which are "parallel" in the life of the nontheist to the theological faith of the traditional believer. This simple change meant that many young men subject to the draft could qualify for alternative civilian service as conscientious objectors, instead of facing ultimate prosecution as draft refusers.

The lesson for future generations of Ethical Humanists should be obvious. Without an organized movement to represent our rights of conscience before the forums and tribunals of government, those rights even in a democratic state will inevitably erode.

Ethical Issues that Leave Room for Honest Differences

Pacifism and conscientious objection to participation in war offer an example of an ethical issue on which people of profound ethical principle can sharply disagree. Many have served honorably in combat because they have felt called upon to fight as a moral obligation. Others, with an equal sense of obligation to do the right, have suffered imprisonment, or—in some countries—even execution, for their commitment to nonviolence. Unlike such matters of clear principle as racial equality, on which virtually all Ethical Humanists and other people of good will are agreed, there are other issues, such as pacifism, where all do not agree. On such matters, the Ethical Humanist movement supports the moral right and duty of individuals to follow their consciences, without violating the rights of others.

One such issue that divides the nation is capital punishment. In their time Felix Adler, John L. Elliott, and Henry Neumann were prominent among Ethical leaders working to abolish the taking of life as a punishment for crime. Later, Jerome Nathanson headed the New York Committee to Abolish Capital Punishment, with offices of the committee provided at the New York society's meeting house. At the present time, with capital punishment being revived in the United States, Joseph Chuman, leader of the Bergen County (New Jersey) society has become a principal activist in state and regional coalitions and groups to oppose reinstatement of the death penalty. Chuman, together with members of several New York area societies, has promoted the work of Amnesty International, an organization active throughout the world on behalf of "prisoners of conscience." Like the American Civil Liberties Union and other constitutional rights groups, Amnesty has shown the racial, sexual, and class bias present in sentences of execution, as well as the use of capital punishment in ideological repression.

Despite these weighty arguments and even in the light of the ethical first principle of the sanctity of every life, some Ethical Humanists are convinced that capital punishment is justifiable and necessary. They argue that mentally competent persons must be responsible for their acts and that when those acts involve premeditated murder the guilty must forfeit their own lives. Otherwise, it is argued, we would punish every crime except the most heinous of all crimes, especially when the offender may be under a life sentence for other acts of violence.

The example serves to remind us that thoughtful, morally committed people may reach opposing or even sharply antagonistic conclusions. The function of democracy is to make possible the free interchange of all opinions in a moral environment of mutual respect and forebearance. Out of such "dialogue" moral persuasion, if not ultimate truth, may be advanced.

In such ways and for such causes as we have described above, the Ethical Humanist movement labors to maintain—in V. T. Thayer's phrase—"an ethical conception of democracy," to advance an open and pluralistic society where differences of belief and conscience, like differences of race, culture, and ideology, are protected and cultivated rather than persecuted, where differences are understood to enrich community rather than to disrupt it. Principled dissent and nonconformity are the necessary regenerators of ethical democracy—the only form of democracy that is more than skin deep.

Summarizing More Than a Century of Social Action and Service

From its inception, the Ethical movement has striven to live the ideal of "deed above creed." All that we have recorded in the preceding pages and chapters offers only a bare and necessarily incomplete rendering of the many practical demonstrations of the working faith of Ethical Humanism. For in having turned away from the speculative and purely verbal activity of the Free Religious Association, Adler sought to make his Ethical Culture movement an embodiment of ethics in action. The history of the movement shows how remarkably he succeeded: The first settlement house in America (now the University Settlement of New York), established only ten years after the Society itself; kindred programs in Philadelphia and St. Louis; the beginnings, even earlier, of the first free kindergartens in New York and Chicago; the District Nursing Service that grew into the Visiting Nurse Service; the Tenement House Building Company to upgrade the quality of housing for the poor; the United Relief Works of the New York Society, now the United Social Services; the Workingmen's School, now the Ethical Culture Schools of New York; the Working Boys Club of the Philadelphia Society; the Self-Culture Halls Association of St. Louis (where civil libertarian Roger Baldwin began his career of social education and action);

the Visiting and Teaching Guild for Crippled Children of New York; the Hudson Guild and Hudson Guild Farm, providing vocational training and other social services for young people and families of the tenement district of Manhattan's "Hell's Kitchen"; the Summer School of Ethics at Madison, Wisconsin, with Anna Garlin Spencer as Director; the Committee of Fifteen, including Felix Adler, to end gross corruption in New York City government; and the International Congress on Moral Education. These undertakings are only a sample of the many programs and agencies launched by the Ethical movement, or by its leaders, or by groups of lay members. To tell more would require a much longer book, and to make the record complete would require a library.

In the present generation one can find many comparable, and usually unsung, expressions of Ethical Humanist faith in action. (Let it be noted that the present is often overly awed by the early record, while less than fully cognizant of more recent and ongoing accomplishments—an array impressive enough if one bothers to assemble it!) Without boasting of the work of our own generation, we can mention the devotion of the group (principally women) who still serve as a volunteer staff at the United Nations headquarters in New York, representing the International Humanist and Ethical Union; the painstaking and sometimes hazardous action taken over many years to advance the cause of Civil Rights and racial equality in both north and south; the notable accomplishments of Algernon D. Black, which include organizing and leading the New York and National Committees Against Discrimination in Housing and related equal-opportunity initiatives; the work for prison reform and the restoration of ex-prisoners to useful roles in society; the struggle to secure freedom of conscience for religious minorities and the nonreligious; the continuing effort through church-state committees and interfaith coalitions to preserve the separation of church and state; the successful effort to end the legal disqualification of nontheistic conscientious objectors under Selective Service law as related above; the Center for Applied Ethics of the New York Society, which addressed questions of business, professional, and governmental ethics—and that helped shape the Ethics in Government Act of the Carter administration; the shelters-for-the-homeless programs of several societies during the years following governmental reductions in aid; the movementwide struggle for abortion rights and equal rights for women; the campaign for peace and mutual arms reduction; the ongoing work to build bridges of communication and understanding in our local communities and, through the IHEU, in "dialogues" across the ideological barriers of East and West. If these latter-day concerns and involvements seem to be of a more ad hoc and "networking" character than the institutional and well-funded programs of the past, this difference reflects current conditions, modes of organization, and utilization of more limited resources during an era of rising costs and high taxes, rather than a slackening of imagination or will.

Ethical Humanism places the emphasis of its social work on the ideal of democracy as the ethical way of life. As we have argued, democracy is social, educational, cultural, and economic, just as it is also political. Indeed, political democracy is not viable unless the other aspects of democracy are also present. Accordingly, the concept of "charity" has always been inadequate as a foundation for the community service of an Ethical movement dedicated to "the ethical conception of democracy." Ethical Humanism's maxim for social action therefore becomes: We must reach out to empower the best in others, even as we seek to expend the best in ourselves.

CHAPTER NINE

The Humanist Way for
Community and Personal Living

T he test of a philosophy is in the living. In an adage
attributed to Jesus, the New Testament puts the matter somewhat more colorfully: "By their fruits ye shall know
them."

Human character is described in images of contrasting
botanical species: "Do men gather grapes of thorns, or figs
of thistles?" Trees that produce evil fruit, we are assured,
will be cut down and destroyed.

We do not require an orthodox conception of divine
wrath, whether in this life or hereafter, to appreciate the
stark realism of the concluding moral of the story. If the
pudding is insipid or unwholesome, it will go into the gar-
bage pail. And such must be the fate of a morally deficient
philosophy or faith that contends for human loyalty. If it
is adequate to the test of guiding and strengthening our
everyday living, if it can sustain us in the face of the crises
and tragedies that are the inevitable human lot, we will
cling to it as "a good tree" giving shelter and sustenance,
otherwise we will not. When put to this test, how does Ethical Humanism fare as a faith to live by?

Those who do not know Ethical Humanism as a personal
life commitment are often quick to dismiss it without even

the courtesy of a hearing as a weak reed unable to sustain our weight or even to regard it as a poisonous weed and a "menace" to civilization. This is especially true of a multitude of the conventionally minded pious. What else can "right-thinking" folk suppose, given their theological assumptions, of a religion that does not begin with faith in God as an unquestioned (and unquestionable) first principle?

But fortunately for the good name of Ethical Humanism, there are still many fair-minded people, including many religious Jews and Christians, who freely express admiration and gratitude for the ethical lives of the Humanists and freethinkers in their midst. They acknowledge that people known to be humanistic in religious attitude—a decided minority in the American population—contribute disproportionately to the progress and well-being of the nation and world. The demagogic fundamentalist evangelists may have labeled Humanism as "the most dangerous religion in America," but those who are familiar with the lives and accomplishments of Humanists will never believe them.

The "proof" of the Ethical Humanist pudding is in the richness of the individual lives of those who are inspired by this still little-known religious philosophy. It is not a boast to observe that as a group they—and the groups of religious liberals, secularists, and others who most closely resemble them in personal values and community attitudes—have made an impact on democratic life and thought that is exceptional for a minority so small in numbers.

This was brought forcefully to my consciousness more than twenty years ago when I traveled to Montgomery, Alabama, in answer to Martin Luther King's call for thousands of Americans to assemble to protest the crushing of civil rights by Alabama state authorities and police. My friend of many years, James Reeb, with whom I had

worked to organize religious liberal and Humanist par-
ticipation in previous civil-rights demonstrations in
Washington, had been bludgeoned to death in Selma,
Alabama.

I was on a picket line at the White House on a bitterly
cold morning when the radio flashed the news of Jim's
mortal injury. Many others on that interfaith, interracial
line knew Jim as a liberal minister and community activist.
But I also knew him to be an example of that still rare
breed, members of the clergy who are open and enthusiastic advocates of religious Humanism. He was active in
the Unitarian Universalist church and I was leader in the
Ethical Culture movement, but I knew our religious philosophies to be virtually identical. When shortly after Jim's
death President Johnson addressed the nation in one of
his most eloquent and decisive addresses, I noted his predictable reference to "the man of God" who had be mar-
tyred at Selma. Jim, in truth was a "man of Humanity" and
about as theological in his thinking and vocabulary as a
meeting of the local ACLU—where very likely he was in
attendance. Yet, the presidential compliment, "man of
God," was posthumously suitable if God can be taken as a
symbol for the generative and healing power of consecrated
human living.

That Jim Reeb's humanistic devotion was not exceptional
among Humanists and like-minded religious liberals was
dramatized by what I witnessed when I arrived in Montgomery on the morning of the great march that King had
assembled. We were transported to an athletic field outside
the city. A federal court order restricted to a small number
those permitted to march from the scene of the Selma dev-
astation to the state capitol in Montgomery. We—some
thirty thousand—had to await the arrival of the Selma
marchers for the final triumphal procession through the
streets of the city where King's crusade had begun a decade
before.

As I waited in the mud and drizzle of the Alabama field, I began to see familiar faces in the gathering throng, first one, then another, and finally whole groups of friends and coworkers that I had known in former years in Florida, California, Texas, Oklahoma, Oregon, and Washington state. I encountered people I had worked with at a summer camp for disadvantaged youth in New England, acquaintances from New York, New Jersey, Pennsylvania, Ohio, Illinois, Missouri, Kansas, Virginia, Maryland, the District of Columbia, Louisiana, the Carolinas, and Georgia. And so the morning went. We had gathered—Ethical Humanists, religious liberals, varied religious dissenters in our respective communities—for an unexpected family reunion of American Humanists and religious liberals!

To say that only Humanists had answered King's call would be grossly unfair. There were many religious groups identified by their banners: Catholics, Anglicans, Methodists, Jews, Quakers, and secularists, all brought together by a black Baptist preacher named King! But the disproportionately large gathering of those who represented humanistic groups or organizations underscored a truth I already knew about our spiritual fellowship: Humanists are people whose numbers may seem insignificant statistically; but on the front lines where the battles are fought to vindicate human dignity and democratic values, Humanists count! While all faiths answered Martin Luther King's call, it is not amiss to observe that had other Americans responded in the same proportion, the population of Alabama that day would at least have doubled. This was no statistical oddity. The law of averages had not mysteriously broken down. Humanists and like-minded religious liberals were only doing what they have always done, quietly and unnoticed, and what they continue to do today—for civil rights and equal opportunity, for economic justice and good government, for international understanding and world peace, for human well-being and community service.

So much for the baleful influence of America's "most dangerous religion!"

Great Lives Shaped by Concern for Others

If a stranger were to ask the average Ethical Humanist to name the person, leader, or lay member who during the previous half century has most completely lived the community conscience of the Ethical movement, the chances are likely that the reply would be, "Al Black." No other member or leader of Ethical culture has made an impact on the American social conscience equal to that of Algernon D. Black; and no other person, it is safe to say, has shaped the idealism of so many, particularly the young. For an Ethical Humanist at large in the American community, especially in the world of race relations or social action, the name of Ethical Culture most often evokes public familiarity with the figure of Al Black. No other Ethical leader since the death in 1942 of the widely respected John Elliott has awakened the admiration of so many.

Now living in active retirement as leader emeritus of the New York society, over a sixty-year span Black has served as Ethics teacher in the schools, youth worker in the society and at Hudson Guild, a senior leader in New York, director of the Encampment for Citizenship, and a host of other roles in the Ethical movement. These many posts did not inhibit his labors in the wider community, including years of service as a leading member of the board of directors of the National Association for the Advancement of Colored People and a welcomed champion of their cause. In the previous chapter we noted his accomplishment in founding the New York Committee Against Discrimination in Housing and subsequently his part in founding the national committee for the same purpose.

Eleanor Roosevelt not only numbered Al Black among her personal circle of coworkers for racial equality, but she so highly regarded his work in bringing young people together in interracial summer camps for democratic education that she annually received participants in the Encampment for Citizenship at the Roosevelt home at Hyde Park.

As a protégé of John Elliott, founder and head worker of Hudson Guild, the young Al Black had gone to work in the slums, befriending youth of every race, calling upon distressed old people who withered in the gloom behind gray tenement windows, running their errands and seeking help for medical and legal needs, and all the while educating himself to the social and material requirements of a viable democratic society. After completing his degree in economics at Harvard, Black, who had been a scholarship student of the Ethical Culture Schools since early childhood, gravitated back to the movement and city that had molded his character and prepared him for his life's work.

When Adler died in 1933, the mantle of senior leadership fell on John Elliott who had worked in the Ethical movement, both at the Society and at Hudson Guild since the 1890s. Black was Elliott's kind of leader, and a year after Elliott's appointment, he inducted the thirty-three-year-old Black into the leadership. As a youth of poor immigrant parentage, Black understood firsthand the nature of ethnic and racial prejudice. In the mid-thirties, with Elliott's full support, Black became an outspoken opponent of Fascism, this at a time when many "conservative" Americans enthusiastically welcomed Mussolini, Hitler, and Franco as the saviors of Western civilization from communism. (At the time strong fascistic organizations existed in the United States, including metropolitan New York and New Jersey, agitating for the U.S. to follow the German and Italian example.) In this setting Black's radio broadcasts became a focal point of moral vigilance for democratic survival.

When race riots swept Harlem in 1941, he joined with an interracial group of community leaders to organize the Citizen's Committee for Harlem. Other Ethical leaders throughout the country followed a similar course. For example, when a few years later Dr. George Beauchamp became the first leader of the recently organized society in Washington, D.C., he became a force for the elimination of racial segregation in the nation's capital. Following in the same footsteps, when segregationist resistance to civil rights was at its height, lay members Anita and Robert Stein, with Ethical leader Walter Lawton, undertook at the peril of their lives organization of integrated summer play schools in the deep south.

The energetic commitment of Ethical Humanists to social justice, exemplified in the work of Elliott, Black, Beauchamp, Lawton, and the Steins, should not be interpreted as primarily ideological or political—except insofar as loyalty to human dignity can be called the ideology of basic Humanist morality. Indeed, if one took these representative figures—or any three or four other Ethical Humanists—it is unlikely that they would be in agreement politically. But they would agree on the right of all human beings to a life of decency in a community in which all are treated as of equal worth.

In the moral and spiritual anthropology of Ethical Humanism, dignity and moral freedom are defining characteristics of being fully human. As we help to activate these human attributes in other lives, we rally our own deeper qualities of personhood. Again, we confront in practice the validity of the Adlerian ethical maxim, this time rephrased descriptively: As you have acted to empower the greater personhood of others, so you have actualized a fuller personhood in yourself.

The Ethical Function of Vocation in Workplace and Government

Among the seminal concepts of Adler's thought that have been too much neglected, even by Ethical Humanists, is his conception of the moral significance of vocation. In Adler's thinking, work was more than economic activity. The doctrine of vocation as he developed it has a long and honored religious history, going back to the ancient and medieval ideas of ordination, or consecration, for performance of some sacred obligation. The religious orders were regarded as such spiritual "vocations," when monks or nuns dedicated themselves to lives of labor for the glorification of their faith.

Taking the idea out of its theological dress, Adler recognized the value of the spiritual conception of vocation as an instrument for personal and social growth. He conceived of the organization of society along vocational lines, in which the various professions and industries would be extensions of the ideal of mutual service. While no overall social reconstruction such as Adler envisaged has been feasible under existing economic structures, Ethical Culturists have attempted to apply his thought to their personal occupations. From time to time movement-sponsored conferences and institutes have attempted to study patterns of industrial organization and practice as well as professional and governmental ethics with the aim of proposing practical measures to lessen moral conflicts.

Adler himself brought together groups of businessmen and professionals to discuss ethical practices and abuses in their work. A former president of the New York society, Sidney Scheuer, a businessman of international prominence in the textile industry, and an official in charge of wartime trade in the Roosevelt administration, remembers the influence these discussions had upon him as a young participant.

Adler proposed to establish a school of applied ethics to address industrial and professional ethics, and while a formal institution for that purpose has not been created, a number of ad hoc programs have been organized by the Ethical movement, principally by the New York Society. At least two such efforts deserve mention.

In 1943, when democratic thinkers were beginning to look ahead to the shape of the future after the approaching end of World War II, Jerome Nathanson of the New York Society's Board of Leaders convened the first Annual Conference on Science and Democracy. (Earlier we encountered Nathanson as a prime mover in introducing into Ethical Culture John Dewey's philosophy of humanistic naturalism.) Nathanson was inspired to call the conference after reflecting on Dewey's emphasis on the impact of science in shaping contemporary society. He received Dewey's enthusiastic support for the undertaking. Subsequent conferences followed in 1944 and 1945. The published papers of the three conferences, which had drawn a prestigious gathering of scientists and social philosophers, highlighted technological development, social and moral change, economic and industrial evolution, and the beginnings of the global wave of nationalism that has grown ever stronger in the emerging cultures.

In 1972, the New York Society sponsored creation of the Center for Applied Ethics, which Society president Ivan Shapiro and I had earlier proposed without knowing of the other's initiative. Over an eight-year period the Center established five successive working groups, or "think tanks," of expert participants, unpaid volunteers, the majority of whom are recruited from beyond the society membership. These panels specialized in the fields of financial securities, the finance of medical services, law, the regulation of safe nuclear power, and conflicts of interest resulting from the "revolving door" between government office and industrial employment. Two of the studies (delivery of health care, and nuclear power safety) resulted in major conferences that influenced leading figures in their fields. Two other panels had even more far-ranging effects.

The published study and recommendations that resulted from the panel on conflicts of interest in the financial securities industry were reported in *The New York Times, The*

Wall Street Journal, and *Newsday,* and circulated by mailings from the Center to business schools and federal and state regulatory agencies. State agencies in Wisconsin and Connecticut used the findings in reviewing their regulatory measures, and the material found its way into business-school ethics classes. (As director of the Center, I was invited to serve as a consultant to a Massachusetts business college in setting up its ethical education program.) Our panel was invited to make presentations at meetings of the New York Society of Security Analysts and to a panel of the New York Stock Exchange.

In the early months of the Carter administration I was invited to the White House by the Counsel to the President, Robert Lipshutz, to confer on ethics in government-industrial relations. As a result, the Center was invited to submit recommendations to accomplish reforms that President Carter was determined to make in order to deter conflicts of interest. Our study, made by a group chaired by Ivan Shapiro, which I coordinated, brought a second invitation (this time to the panel as a whole) to present our findings to the President's Counsel and his associate at the White House. The Counsel urged us to submit our recommendations to the Senate Governmental Operations Committee, then drafting provisions of the Ethics in Government Act. Shortly after our return to New York, I received a call from the Senate committee's chief counsel. He asked me to return to Washington for consultation, saying our report was the most useful of any presented during the Senate hearings. Thus, Felix Adler's dream of the systematic examination of ethical practices in vocational and business life made an ultimate impact on the Ethics Act of 1977.

While such public consequences may be rare, the influence of ethical sensitivity in our individual vocational lives can be a steady source of satisfaction, bringing a sense of worth to the workplace. Don Robert Johnson, senior leader of the New York society, has written that in his work he finds personal vocational fulfillment when three factors converge: recognition of a particular need in the broader community; confidence about one's abilities and talents in relation to that need; and a desire and passion towards this work. Meaningful productive life thus involves a fusion of moral passion with a sense of useful labor.

The Qualities of Spiritual Wholeness in Personal Living

Throughout this volume we have emphasized the social foundations of personality development. Each of us is the outcome of a social "project" initially directed by others; who continue throughout our lives to exert a shaping influence. We do not have the privilege of designing human personality to have it meet our favored specifications. When we try, we do violence to the material and risk creating a victim or a monster. Everything we have said throughout this book about the creative process that generates human personality should have underscored that fact.

The primary place of the family, and a high commitment to the vows of marriage as a sexually exclusive and permanent bond, furnished the cornerstone of Adler's conception of the moral structure of human society. While Ethical Humanist thinking on marriage and the roles of the sexes has undergone considerable change in the period since Adler addressed the issues, Ethical Humanists maintain their concern that this integral and formative relationship should remain central as the principal child-rearing unit and should continue to express the most complete and nurturing relationship in the lives of men and women. At the same time, the adequacy of any existing marital institution must be measured against its consistency with the overriding principle of the equality of sexes, the equitable distribution of responsibilities and rights, and the individual needs of its members to grow into emotionally mature, loving, and mutually sustaining individuals. Such marriages are not available to everyone, and a tolerant and humanistic culture must recognize the necessity for other possible life patterns and relationships where the same standards of mutuality and caring obtain. At the close of his period of service as senior leader of the New York Society, Dr. Sheldon Ackley observed:

> We are all aware that the so-called nuclear family has only recently developed out of the extended family. There were several major changes in personal life and personal relationships that occurred as a result of this shift. Perhaps the most startling and revolutionary one was the adoption of an ideal of conjugal affection. A new standard was created for relationships between men and women in marriage.

Dr. Ackley argues that with the further evolution of the concept of marriage and the movement toward equality between the sexes, the ideal of "conjugal affection," of love as the basis of the marital partnership, has become progressively strengthened. The adequacy of marriage patterns in this changed environment must be measured against their capacity to satisfy the requirement of equality and to provide a suitable framework for sustaining loving relationships. To the extent that contemporary marriage fails to meet these needs, changes are necessary. And alternative patterns and relationships that further these values must be countenanced. In arguing these modifications in social mores, Dr. Ackley and other Ethical Humanists are not suggesting that personal responsibility and fidelity can be ignored. On the contrary, the moral demand that Ethical Humanism requires of sexual relationships, including marriage and family, is that responsible mutuality be observed more consistently and fairly.

Personal Relationships and Mental Health

Students of the typology of religious movements sometimes distinguish between two primary psychological emphases in the various faiths, the psychocentric and the sociocentric. Those sects that look primarily inward, concentrating on the state of the inner consciousness with little attention to the moral and social dimensions of life, are classified as psychocentric. Those, in contrast, that focus on community relationships and social reforms—the "social-gospel" type of religion—are dubbed sociocentric. A complete religious philosophy capable of seeing life whole must of course contain both elements. The social dimension and the private inner life are the necessary poles of a unified field of moral and spiritual experience.

While the history of the Ethical Humanist movement would suggest a "tilt" in the direction of the social aspect of religion—and Humanists would not be apologetic about this emphasis on "deed" in their faith—the feeding of the inner life is no less important. What Ethical Humanists insist upon is that the inner life of the individual self and the interpersonal context of life are inseparable aspects of a living whole. We cannot be "spiritual" apart from the human and natural environment. We are linked to all that lives, in consciousness as in material and biological kinship. This truth is just as fundamental for mental health and a fulfilling emotional life as it is for social ethics.

Ethical Humanist philosophers and spiritual leaders are alert to the growing excesses of selfishness and egocentricity in contemporary life. The popular notion that a human being can find "fulfillment" and personal satisfaction by self-centered pursuits, won at the expense of spouses, children, coworkers, and neighbors, is one that we emphatically reject. The cure for guilt-ridden subservience to others, for being victimized by a martyr complex, is not abandonment of nurturing family relationships and obligations for the sake of a fling of "independence." Those who abandon life's deepest ties and commitments to "have it all" usually end with less than they had before.

Happiness in any enduring, meaningful sense is the outcome of growth to personal maturity. And the way to maturity is not through the parched desert of self-serving ruthlessness and contempt for others—especially for those closest to us in kinship and need. Hopelessly bad and exploitive relationships are better ended than endured. But always in the disruption of long-established ties and bonds of trust there are profound and lasting personal losses, both to ourselves and to others. Lives are truncated in the breaking of linkages that define us as individuals or that sever the emotional lifelines that we have provided to those who need us most.

Near the end of his life Professor Joseph L. Blau, then the most philosophically distinguished member of the Ethical Humanist leadership, voiced a caution against the drift of the past half-century toward "a formlessness that is not mere fluidity, but has gone beyond fluidity toward chaos." He contrasted this steady disintegration of the vessels and channels of the moral life with the reconstructive purpose of the Ethical movement. From the beginning Ethical Culture abandoned inadequate and obsolete patterns only for the sake of replacing them with a more adequate moral plan. Always the freedom of the individual and responsibility to the social group had to be brought into harmony:

> One explicit intention of the creators of our Movement was to leave more room for new meaning to be expressed, more space in which individuals could grow, to be creative. The group, the society, was to be a place where such creativity could be accepted and even tested in practice. But we

must remember that behind this ideal, supporting it and
buttressing it, was the equally explicit concern to develop
an ethic that linked social and individual concerns, and,
therefore, could not place the ideal of self-expression above
the primary goals of the group. . . . What I can do is to help
others toward realizing their potential for giving the same
kind of individualized help to me and to still others.

Such an ethical principle is worlds removed from the
cult of self-indulgence that some contemporary self-help
"experts" peddle in the marketplace of popular psychology
and journalism. That these fads are sometimes confused
in the media with Humanism is a cause of particular pain
to those Ethical Humanist writers and thinkers who have
always emphasized Humanism's interpersonal and social
conception of personality development and ethics. Prominent among these is James F. Hornback, recently retired
as leader of the St. Louis Ethical Society and a former
president of the American Ethical Union and former chair
of the National Leaders Council. Hornback, who has also
played a leading role in the American Humanist Association, protests vigorously the practice of many uninformed
writers and religious critics to confuse ethical and philosophical Humanism with the "me-first" attitude of popular
cultural faddism.

For more than a generation the acknowledged dean of
mental health work and family counseling in the Ethical
Humanist movement has been Matthew Ies Spetter, who
with boundless energy has combined a career as leader of
the Riverdale-Yonkers (N.Y.) society with close involvement
with the Riverdale Mental Health Clinic, which he founded
in 1960. (We have already told of his brush with death at
the hands of the Nazis—his execution having been aborted
only by accident.) In addition to his leadership duties and
counseling, Dr. Spetter managed to find time to chair the
Ethics Department at the Ethical Culture School and to

teach peace education studies at a Riverdale college, among other teaching obligations.

Spetter's approach to life-values education and counseling has combined the professional skill and theory of a sociologist and social psychologist with the moral and spiritual insights of a minister of religious Humanism. Equally at home with the writings of contemporary theologians, existentialist philosophers, and the social criticism of thinkers as diverse as Camus, Tillich, Fromm, Michael Harrington, and Father John Cronin, he has rejected the superficial optimism of much recent liberal and "humanistic" opinion, insisting instead that courage in the face of certain suffering and loss is the foundation of mental health and moral resiliency. As a survivor of both Auschwitz and Buchenwald, who lost his family to Nazi atrocities, Spetter sees freedom as a strength to be won through effort and struggle, not as a prize to be selfishly consumed.

In the same vein, he affirms with Erich Fromm the active and productive orientation that sustains relationships of love and marriage, while purely self-assertive behaviors and interests defeat our life-loving drives. We are born with the need to be needed, with the need to reach out to others to satisfy that hunger of our social natures:

> Is it not time to accept as anthropologists, child-psychiatrists and educators already do, that the concept that the child is born egocentric is a projection of our own conditioning as adults? The facts are that the newborn infant's organism is already an actively cooperating entity. Hostility in children tends to increase as they grow older, for aggression is the response to deprivation of tenderness.

Spetter concludes that on scientific grounds we have confirmed the common observation that "We learn to love by having been loved. Actually, compassionate feelings are the basis of every coherent society." A society that is built on the moral philosophy of Ethical Humanism cannot foster the self-hate and contempt for others that come from denying the social foundations of human existence. He writes:

> A civilization, in which individuals not only stick together for mutual protection or self-interest, but in which they share specific ideals and purpose, is a civilization of love in which hostility and fear of the future have been replaced by supportive aims. There is no doubt that such a world community is possible and may be probable.

A summary of Spetter's moral psychology is perhaps encapsulated adequately in a sentence from his book, *Man, the Reluctant Brother,* from which the quotations above are also taken: "Compassion and love are in their very essence social phenomena, values to be aspired to as definitely 'good', since they tie the self in with the preservative needs of all."

Ethical leader Judith Espenschied supports the conclusion that ethical values have a validity that can be put to the test, making them objective in the same sense that the "hard" sciences are objective. John Dewey would have agreed since in his theory moral principles are generalizations based on predictions of probable outcomes, making them comparable to the hypotheses of the positive sciences.

"Maybe it is not true," reasons Espenschied, "that the subject matter of ethics is immeasurable and unscientific. Maybe it is just complex, and harder to quantify. . . . Hard science may just be easy by comparison." In any case, she argues:

> Ethics is a necessary, integral, and perhaps not incommensurable part of our world. It is built into our educational and social and family and economic and cultural systems.

We might dispense with hard science, as many primitive societies have done. But we could not eliminate ethics.

The Unity of Ethical Theory and Personal Living

Speaking for the younger generation of leaders at the Centennial observance of the Ethical Culture movement, Donald Montagna of the Washington, D.C., society, voiced their common determination to bring a closer relationship between the social conscience of Ethical Culture and the effort to strengthen the personal relationships of people in the societies. Cultivation of warmth and caring for each other, a more deeply felt sense of being members of a gathered community, rather than an outer-directed emphasis on "saving the world," should be given greater priority in the movement's second century.

Montagna was not suggesting that Ethical Culture should abandon its social activism or forsake the public concerns that have made the movement an influence far larger than its numbers would suggest. But, he argued, with the weakening of the traditional resources of family and stable communities people in a swiftly changing, fluid culture need greater social reinforcement from their peers than traditional forms of organization and activity provided. This too is a necessary measure for human survival. Finding the appropriate balance between the sociocentric and the psychocentric—serving the activist, reforming cause, while at the same time nurturing the mutual, internal needs of an organized community, must remain a continuing challenge. Ethical Humanism recognizes the just and essential claims of both aspects of our social feeling and life experience.

For Dr. Spetter, the dynamic relationship of tenderness and love with the larger purposes of humanistic civilization furnishes a solution to the problem. John Hoad, present leader of the St. Louis society, makes a similar connection

between the socioeconomic and political macrocosm of the
world at large and the microcosm of personal maturation
through the nurturing resources of good social and family
relationships. Drawing from his experience as a family relations counselor, Hoad interprets the religious philosophy
of Ethical Humanism in the light of advancing therapeutic
insight as well as through the accumulated philosophical
wisdom of the ages.

Attention to the demands for inner psychological nur-
ishment and spiritual renewal does not suggest moral es-
capism to Lois Kellerman, leader of the Queens and
Brooklyn societies, if such attention offers time for needed
reflection and serves as "a prelude to new action as we
journey on." We must distinguish between escapist digres-
sions and energizing repose:

> Sometimes we hide from our demons, our fears, some-
> times we hide from the good. Let us distinguish between
> two kinds of hiding places. Bad hiding places divert us, im-
> prison our mind and hearts, and make us ultimately, un-
> faithful to the past and future. Good hiding places, on the
> other hand, heal, renew, and recommit us in faith to our
> past and future.
>
> I call these good hiding places "sanctuary," places that
> heal. We build private and public sanctuaries in our life as
> a way of making room for the future, of negotiating greater
> goodness which is not yet real in the larger world of our
> lives. Escape is ultimately refuge from reality, driving us to
> momentary pleasure and diversion. In contrast, sanctuary
> at its best creates a holding place for the highest in us, a
> place for moments of personal affirmation.

For Ethical Humanist leader Michael Franch, following
in the tradition of Thoreau and Schweitzer, ethical maturity
comes with learning to live in harmony with the earth
around us, to simplify our needs, and to give thought to

such basic matters as food and clothing. Do we live in such a way as to avoid thoughtless, needless violence against the planet's biosphere, to reverence the will to live of even the humbler species, and to impose the least burden upon the resources of an earth that belongs not to us but to all generations to come? Do we set a good example to others and to our children by our way of living? Following in the same thought, Judy Toth, leader of the Baltimore society, writes: "The primary ethical teaching of all time is 'to cause no unnecessary harm.' Cultivating ecological consciousness then means gaining a greater understanding of how to interact with nature in a positive and creative fashion."

These are a few of the ways in which the vocationally active leaders of the Ethical Humanist movement strive to vivify their religious philosophy in their personal and professional relationships, to make the "deed" of daily behavior the practical embodiment of a faith committed to life's meaning and worth.

Susan Bagot, leader of the Northern Virginia society, sums it up for her colleagues with the observation that our moral commitments must refute the slander often made against liberal religion that "anything goes." On the contrary, "liberal" simply means free, especially pertaining to the mind or soul of the free. As we hope this volume has amply shown, only those can be free who nurture freedom in mutually creative, life-enhancing association with their fellow travelers on this space ship, Earth.

The ethics of Humanism is based on a truth of moral creativity so simple that we can reduce it to one word: mutuality. But human development involves a process so rich in possibilities that we would not be able to describe it fully in a whole library. Such is the immensity of Ethical Humanism's spiritual potential.

Afterword: How to Learn More About Ethical Humanism

W e have now arrived at the conclusion of our survey of Ethical Humanism as a living faith. But this is not the end of our story. After more than a century of spiritual and material development, the Ethical movement remains a vital and creative center of Humanist thought and service. Its capacity for philosophical and moral growth is continuously enhanced, as it gains experience and confidence in the Humanist way of life.

The reader who desires to explore further this unique ethical and religious faith may wish to read further on the philosophy and history of the Ethical movement. Howard B. Radest's book, *Toward Common Ground: The Story of the Ethical Societies in the United States* (Frederick Ungar Publishing Co., New York, 1969), is the authoritative history of the movement's first seventy-five years. This well-researched volume, written by a historian and educator who has served Ethical Culture for a third of a century as leader, former executive of the American Ethical Union, recent Secretary General of the International Humanist and Ethical Union, and current Director of the Ethical Culture Schools of New York, includes personal interviews with many of the leaders and lay members who knew Felix Adler and other figures of the early movement.

Horace L. Friess, late professor of philosophy and religion at Columbia University—instrumental in founding Columbia's Department of Religion which he served as its first chairman—wrote a graceful and insightful biography of Ethical Culture's founder, *Felix Adler and Ethical Culture: Memories and Studies* (Columbia University Press, New York, 1981). Friess, who married Adler's daughter, Ruth, and knew Adler for the final fifteen years of his life, recalled his life and work with an appreciative eye that combined intellectual and personal admiration with judicious critical detachment.

In addition to the books cited above as introductory to the Ethical movement, the serious student of religious Humanism should be familiar with the writings of the late Sir Julian Huxley, especially *Religion Without Revelation* and several later volumes containing essays on Humanism, published by Harper & Row. Also, John Dewey's small classic, *A Common Faith*, first published by Yale University Press in 1934 and since reprinted, makes the case for religious Humanism within the framework of a philosophy of thoroughgoing naturalism.

Readers who seek a more detailed background to the current attack on Humanism by the Radical Religious Right, and the threat their assault poses to the separation of church and state, may wish to consult my book, *American Freedom and the Radical Right* (Frederick Ungar Publishing Co., New York, 1982).

Perhaps I may also be permitted to cite my book on the perennial struggle for intellectual and religious freedom, told through the lives and thought of sixteen representative freethinkers and Humanist precursors from ancient to contemporary times, *The Free Mind Through the Ages* (Frederick Ungar Publishing Co., New York, 1985).

The transcendentalist philosophy of Ralph Waldo Emerson, instrumental in preparing the way for both Ethical Culture and religious Humanism in the United States, is presented in four selected essays from Emerson, which I edited and introduced as a volume in the series, "Milestones of Thought," the Ungar Publishing Company's widely used bookshelf of great thinkers, entitled *Emerson on Transcendentalism* (New York, 1986).

The American Ethical Union, headquartered in the landmark meeting house of the New York Society for Ethical Culture (Central Park West at 64th Street, New York, NY, 10023), is prepared to respond to inquiries on Ethical Humanism and to provide information on available books and literature. The AEU also maintains a membership-at-large program with periodic mailings for those who live in areas that are not served by an Ethical society or fellowship. The New York society also currently houses the Humanist Institute, a leadership training school sponsored on a co-operative basis by the North American Committee for Humanism. Participants include trainees of the Ethical Culture movement, the American Humanist Association, the Society for Humanistic Judaism, and ministerial students of the Unitarian Universalist Association, all endeavoring to enrich their common knowledge of the inclusive Humanist movement, its philosophy and history.

When all is said and done, the Humanist way is simply the way of mutual respect, of passionate loyalty to all our human kindred everywhere on this good earth, and appreciation of life as a priceless pearl to be devoutly cherished. The much-maligned Epicurus, a worthy exemplar even after the passage of twenty-three centuries, spoke as truly for us as for himself and his contemporaries:

> I have anticipated thee, Fortune, and guarded myself against all thy secret attacks. We will not give ourselves up as captives to thee or to any other circumstance. But when it is time to go, we will make our departure singing buoyantly a glorious triumph song that WE HAVE LIVED WELL.

Appendix: Testimony Before the Armed Services Committee of the U.S. Senate on the Religious Basis of Ethical Humanist Conscientious Objection

Given on Behalf of the American Ethical Union by Edward L. Ericson, April 17, 1967, S.1432

[The following prepared statement to the Committee was followed by extensive questioning of the witness by the panel, as appears in the official record. For discussion of the effect of this testimony on the legal status of nontheistic religion, see pages 155 ff.]

Mr. Chairman and Members of the Committee:

My name is Edward L. Ericson. I serve as Leader of the Washington Ethical Society at 7750 Sixteenth Street, N.W., a religious corporation chartered under the laws of the District of Columbia. I testify before you today on behalf of the American Ethical Union, a national federation of Ethical Societies (otherwise known as Ethical Culture Societies) with headquarters at 2 West 64th Street, New York City.

The American Ethical Union wishes to be heard at these hearings on the Selective Service Act because we feel that the definition of religion written into the Act in 1948 is unduly limiting and prejudicial toward a religion such as our own.

Although I shall not take up this Committee's time to describe in detail our belief, it may nevertheless be useful, in order to clarify our purpose in testifying, to indicate briefly our distinctive position in religious thought.

We do not profess a formal creed or theology. It is the ethical aspect of religion which we consider to be of central importance and of lasting and universal concern, quite apart from particular theological beliefs. We are not concerned with converting men to a particular doctrine with respect to God, immortality, or prayer, but with raising the quality of human relationships and fostering respect for ethical and spiritual values in human life, which have been immemorially the common concerns of all civilized religions. We have advocated the right of a group so dedicated to represent itself to the community as a religion and to be treated equally with religious bodies of a more traditional and familiar form. In a word, we interpret religion to embrace man's ultimate values or ultimate concerns, which for us are essentially ethical, without necessary dependence upon any particular metaphysical doctrine or theology. (I am appending to this statement a short description of the nature of nontheological religions and of the place which they have occupied in Eastern and Western world cultures.)

Because we feel that the definition of religion as written into the Selective Service Act of 1948 has tended to deny equal treatment to persons and to religious bodies such as ours, we would like to have the provision re-examined by this Committee with a view toward the correction of a bias in the law which has had unfortunate ramifications for us and others. The implications of this limiting definition of religion under American law reach far beyond the context of the Selective Service Act, as I shall try to show in this statement.

The definition to which I refer occurs in the section which defines religion with respect to those who are conscientious objectors to war by reason of religious training and belief. Section 6 (j) declares: "Religious training and belief in this connection means an individual's belief in relation to a Supreme Being involving duties superior to those arising from any human relation, but does not include essentially political, sociological, or philosophical views or a merely personal moral code."

I would like to voice our objections and strong protests to this definition on two counts: (1) Its immediate adverse effect upon young men of sincere, conscientious views whose particular religion or faith is not readily covered by this definition of religion as belief in a Supreme Being, and (2) the more remote and indirect consequences of such a definition under Federal law for religious groups or individuals, which reach beyond the immediate issue of conscientious objection.

We are aware of the fact that the decision of the United States Supreme Court in the case *U.S. vs. Seeger* (March 8, 1965) considerably broadened the legal interpretation of the Supreme Being clause. The effect of this broad construction enabled the Court to sustain the right of a young man to be recognized as a conscientious objector even though he professed to believe in no deity or Supreme Being other than a belief in ethical values as a religious concern. In effect, Seeger professed to believe in ethics in place of God, or in place of a Supreme Being.

Although Seeger was not a member of an Ethical Society, he was affirming a conception of religion which Ethical Culturists have subscribed to since the founding of our first Society ninety-one years ago. During that long history, Ethical Societies have been an accepted part of the religious spectrum in American life, having existed and worked harmoniously side by side with churches, synagogues, and other religious congregations. It was not until a decade or so ago, after the passage of the Act containing the limiting definition of religion already cited, that our right to be a religious body under the law was legally questioned and put to a court test. Although the Ethical Society won that test (*Washington Ethical Society vs. District of Columbia,* United States Court of Appeals, for the District of Columbia Circuit, No. 13,646) and continues to enjoy the protections afforded to religion under the Constitution, it should be brought to the attention of this Committee that the definition of religion given in the Draft law of 1948 was used and has been used in other contexts as an argument against our continued acceptance as a religious body under American legal practice.

Members of this Committee may wonder why we continue to express concern over the wording of this law, now that the courts by a very broad construction have sustained us, as they sustained the conscientious objector, Seeger. The answer to this is at least twofold.

In the first place, law has a moral and social effect reaching beyond what is strictly enforceable. The courts may save us from a harsh or literal reading of the law, and may even express the opinion that to invoke a stricter interpretation would raise serious constitutional problems, as in fact the courts have done, but this does not spare us the obloquy or invidious exclusion which the narrow wording of the law tends to support.

If, for example, the law were written in such terms that a strict interpretation argued against acceptance of Judaism or Catholicism as a religion, I am sure you can understand that the aggrieved minority would protest with good cause and seek a fairer and less prejudicial rendering. It would be of no avail to argue that an anti-Semitic law would be innocuous if unenforceable, or that a disqualification of Catholics would be of no concern if the courts avoided the exclusion. As a historic religious body which has played an honorable part in the growth of religious pluralism and social ethics in American life, the American Ethical Union must protest the continued use in a Federal law of a definition of religion which prefers one class or type of religion (however numerous or familiar) over other conceptions of religion.

In the Torcaso case (*Torcaso vs. Watkins*) in 1961, the U.S. Supreme Court cited Buddhism, Ethical Culture, and Humanism as existing religious groups in the United States founded upon beliefs other than belief in God. (One could cite other examples as well, as noted in the Appendix to this statement.) The Supreme Court in the Seeger case ruled that a parallel belief, such as devotion to an ethical principle or ideal, should be construed as fulfilling the requirement of "belief in a Supreme Being." This, we believe, was the only course which the Court could take without declaring the provision, as written, to be unconstitutional. The Congress, however, has a greater initiative and can correct the defect of the present version by a very simple substitution in wording.

I would note, for example, that the provision in the 1940 Selective Service Act, which served throughout World War II, did not raise many of the problems which have come about since the enactment of the provision of 1948. The simpler (and, we would hold, wiser) wording of the Selective Training and Service Act of 1940 did not attempt to provide a definition of religion, but left this ultimately to judicial interpretation in the light of all relevant social and constitutional considerations.

We do not believe that Congress intended to prefer one class of religion over another, although the consequence of the Supreme Being clause since 1948 has been to open a series of problems for religious minorities which do not conform to the definition of the prevailing type or class of theistic religions which are most numerous and familiar in our country. I am not here to argue that my religion is superior to those religions which are based upon theistic belief. The point is that such a judgment is out of place in governmental deliberations. The purpose of the First Amendment is to forbid such favoritism. I do not come here to argue the merits of a cause, but simply to argue that the Federal government ought not, and constitutionally cannot, take sides.

This issue is not purely academic. For the young man of Ethical Culturist or humanistic religious beliefs, who does not profess to believe in a Supreme Being, as that term is popularly understood, the present wording of the law (even with the Court's ultimate support) often produces discrimination.

Only last month I wrote a letter for a young man of my own religious society who is a conscientious objector. (I point out, for the information of the Committee, that the majority of our members are not pacifists, but that, like most other American religious bodies, a number are; and the American Ethical Union has always upheld the conscientious scruples of even a small minority of its members.) This young man, who turned to me as his clergyman for assistance, had been denied classification for alternative service despite his obvious sincerity. He had interpreted quite literally the question on his Selective Service form about belief in a Supreme Being and had answered negatively. I am pleased that the Selective Service Board reversed its judgment after a hearing in which my letter was read. I pointed out that the terminology "Supreme Being" is not commonly used among us to summarize or describe our ultimate concerns of a spiritual or religious character and that the young man had answered honestly and literally, not being aware of the extended meaning which the term "Supreme Being" has acquired as a result of judicial interpretation. But this case only illustrates the special jeopardy in which youth of our type of religious belief are placed by the wording of the law. Eventual vindication by the courts may be a harrowing and costly experience.

The American Ethical Union does not ask for any special consideration for conscientious objectors who are Ethical Culturists or of similar Humanist religious views. We ask only that such men should not be singled out for discrimination, and we ask also that no definition of religion should be used in this or any other law which has the effect of narrowing or restricting the meaning of religion generally, so as to prefer one particular type or class of religion, whether theistic, pantheistic, or humanistic, over another. We think such definitions are inevitably defective and restrictive and that the courts and administrative agencies, subject to judicial review, must have flexibility to establish the meaningful limits of religion as a legal and constitutional concept. Only then can ideas have free rein and evolve in response to developments in religious thought and cultural change. Although the courts have mitigated the effects of a discriminatory definition which has been detrimental to us in terms of religious equality and constitutional freedom, we appeal to you to establish equal treatment for all religious bodies and opinions in America supported by the clear, inclusive, and unambiguous language of the law itself.

There is another aspect of the problem of the conscientious objector which the present limitations raise. Although the American Ethical Union has sought consistently, by both legislative and judicial means, to establish a broad and inclusive interpretation of religion, we do not believe that a fair standard of respect for conscience and belief in a democracy allows the nation to provide privileges on a basis of religion which are not available to men of good conscience who consider themselves as secularists and who hold to a moral philosophy which in their lives is comparable to a religion.

While a more inclusive definition of religion is important in order to maintain unimpaired the meaning of religious freedom under the First Amendment, both a sense of fair play and an objective reading of the First Amendment compel us to recognize that the religious and the nonreligious citizen are entitled to equal protection of their beliefs and consciences. Any weakening of this equality is in the last analysis detrimental to religion itself, since it corrupts religion and undermines its moral strength. Therefore, the American Ethical Union believes that rights of conscientious objection under Selective Service ought to be extended to those citizens who feel that they cannot honestly represent their beliefs as religious, but who hold to their convictions with equal sincerity and fidelity as a moral philosophy.

The number of such persons in America is not large. It will not lower the standards of conscientious objection, nor open the floodgates to the casual and the insincere, as is sometimes feared. The insincere can always misrepresent their beliefs to meet any test. It is the honest and sincere who are presently disqualified on the basis of their lack of conformity to religious forms and language. We find such exclusion repugnant to American ideals as a pluralistic and free society. Again, it is not a matter of special privileges or indulgences for secularists. It is simply to recognize that their rights of conscience shall be equal under the law.

Finally, I should like to submit in the Appendix to my testimony, three resolutions related to the Selective Service Act, which were enacted by the Board of the American Ethical Union meeting in New York City last January.

Two of these resolutions deal with questions which I have not discussed in my testimony because the positions they record are self-explanatory, and because I know that the case for these positions has been and will be argued in detail by other witnesses representing a variety of organizations. These deal with (1) recognition of conscientious objectors to particular wars, and (2) the development of plans by Congress to return to a system of voluntary recruitment as the usual method of securing manpower for the armed forces. We believe that the draft, as a long-range or continuing feature of American life, is detrimental to free institutions.

Appendix

Resolutions Related to Selective Service:

(1) *Recognition of Non-Theistic Conscientious Objectors*

WHEREAS the Selective Service law now provides for conscientious objection to military service only if based upon "religious training and belief" and defines religion in terms of belief in a "Supreme Being," and

WHEREAS we believe an official theological definition of religion lies beyond the proper province of secular government and violates the First Amendment to the United States Constitution, and

WHEREAS this definition of religion violates the principles of the American Ethical Union, which is a religious movement founded in 1876 and based upon deeply-felt ethical values rather than belief in a Supreme Being, and

WHEREAS many young men of this and similar religious persuasions are sincere conscientious objectors, and

WHEREAS other young men who are sincere conscientious objectors do not define their life-philosophies in religious terms, and

WHEREAS the United States Supreme Court has found that conscientious objection is entitled to legal recognition when based upon a belief that "occupies a place in the life of the possessor parallel to that filled by the orthodox belief in God,"

NOW THEREFORE BE IT RESOLVED that the Congress of

the United States be petitioned to amend the Selective Service Act by removing the clause restricting the definition of religion to belief in a Supreme Being and by making additional provision for conscientious objection based upon philosophical conviction.

(2) *Recognition of Conscientious Objection to Particular Wars*

WHEREAS the development and exercise of individual conscience is encouraged by the highest teachings of the world's greatest philosophies and religions, and

WHEREAS the American legal heritage has honored and protected the highest degree of liberty for the individual conscience, and

WHEREAS the consciences of many men compel them to object to particular wars and military acts even though they do not claim to be absolute pacifists or to object to every war which could conceivably arise, and

WHEREAS the convictions of such men are often just as strong and sincere as the convictions of absolute pacifists and equally deserving of legal recognition,

NOW THEREFORE BE IT RESOLVED that the American Ethical Union call upon Congress to amend the Selective Service Act to provide legal recognition for conscientious objection to particular wars.

(3) *Return to Voluntary Recruitment*

BE IT RESOLVED that the American Ethical Union call upon the President and Congress to develop a plan to end the present draft law and return to the American tradition of relying on voluntary methods of military recruitment except during limited periods of the gravest national emergency.

A Note on Non-Theistic Religions

In its Torcaso decision (*Torcaso vs. Watkins*) the U.S. Supreme Court noted Buddhism, Ethical Culture, and Humanism (designated as "secular humanism," a term which many Religious Humanists would find misleading) as examples within the United States of religions founded upon beliefs other than a belief in God.

In its amicus curiae brief in the case *Washington Ethical Society vs. District of Columbia* (United States Court of Appeals for the District of Columbia Circuit, No. 13,646) the American Ethical Union described the concept of nontheistic religion as it applies to Ethical Culture: "The Ethical Movement may be described as a "nontheistic" religion. The term 'nontheistic' as used by scholars and as used in this brief is not equivalent to and is to be distinguished from 'atheistic.' Atheism makes positive assertions about the nonbeing of God. Theism makes positive assertions to the contrary. In a nontheistic religion, such as the Ethical Movement, the existence of God is neither affirmed nor denied."

A basic pamphlet of the American Ethical Union, *What Is an Ethical Society?* declares: "The Ethical Society occupies the place of a church or synagogue in the lives of most of its members. It differs from traditional religious bodies in that ethical concern rather than theological doctrine constitutes the basis of fellowship. Members may hold to whatever philosophical and religious views impress them as true or reasonable, so long as they recognize the Society's central concern with human relationships: a positive and constructive faith in the values and potentialities of human life in the natural universe."

It has been noted that nontheistic religions have appeared in both Western and Eastern history, although this type of religion is much more familiar in the Orient than in European civilization. Some (but not all) types of Buddhism profess no concept of a deity or supreme being, cultivating instead a sense of spirituality within the lives of the believers. This is true of primitive Buddhism, as taught by its founder, Gautama (who is generally classified as agnostic), and of several schools of Japanese Buddhism, including Zen, which many authorities regard as among the most spiritual of religions in feeling and self-discipline. Confucianism, in its pure form, is another nontheistic belief which is generally classified as both a religion and a philosophy.

The line between religion and philosophy is difficult to draw and cannot be drawn sharply without committing violence to the unity of thought and religious feeling. Sir Julian Huxley, in his classic introduction to humanist religion, *Religion Without Revelation,* identified religion as the sense or sentiment of the sacred. Other thinkers have taken a similar view. Considering a sense of reverence or devotion to some ideal end or spiritual object to be the common element in various religions, Paul Tillich, and theologians following his lead, have pointed to "ultimate concern" as the essence of the religious quest. All of these approaches recognize a wide variety of possible forms which the object or objects of such devotion may take, including a concept of God or gods, devotion to ideal values, or commitment to a spiritual principle or cause.

In the United States, not only Ethical Societies, but also most Unitarian and some other "free" churches, profess no theological creed or confession and admit to membership both "theists" and "humanists."

Index